Passing Reflections
Volume III

SURVIVING SUICIDE LOSS
THROUGH MINDFULNESS

KRISTEN SPEXARTH

Printed in the United States of America.

Visit the book's site at
PassingReflections.com

For information, visit us at Big Think
Media, Inc., www.bigthinkmedia.com, or
contact us at info@bigthinkmedia.com

ISBN: 978-0-9908834-0-1

Dedicated to Loss Survivors

Opened by love and loss,
life's paradox is revealed:
broken brings us whole.

———————————

Life is so beautiful, in its
triumphs and tragedies.
Everywhere I look I see it now.
There is beauty even in fear
and pain, but visible only to
those deeply submerged in it.

- Colby Spexarth

Contents

Acknowledgments

Like many survivors, involvement in outreach has been of benefit, giving me a chance to find healing and meaning through association with the community of loss survivors. Over the years both individuals and non-profit groups have contributed to my education in this regard.

The organizations that have most helped me are: Forefront: Innovations In Suicide Prevention at the University of Washington, Seattle (Forefront); King County Crisis Clinic; and the American Association of Suicidology. These organizations have provided expertise, helping guide my path of healing, as well as afforded me opportunities to contribute to the group effort.

I am also grateful for the people working in the field of suicidology, especially Dr. Melinda Moore of Eastern Kentucky University and Sue Eastgard of Forefront UW. For their tireless activity serving survivors and their significant contributions to the field of suicide pre- and postvention, I offer my sincere admiration and appreciation. For the staff and collaborators working with Forefront, you are an inspiration.

I am grateful beyond words for all who have supported my work with suicide survivor outreach. These include my publisher and editor, Arushi Sinha of Big Think Media, who has championed this work from the beginning and my layout artist, Leslie Lee. Thank you for your skill and enduring enthusiasm. Many thanks also to fellow survivor, Nancy Ross, who made this volume possible, giving me a chance to complete the body of work that began with *Passing Reflections*.

Sincere thanks go to all who helped by reading and commenting on this manuscript, including Robert Carlson, Wendy Carlson, Anabel Cole, Vincent de Rosa, Sue Eastgard, Susan Lebow, Dr. Melinda Moore, Laura Nelson, Jude Rozhon, Charlene Weber, Elizabeth Weber and Karen Weber.

And for my son Arlen and daughter-in-law Anna, I hold you in my heart, as always, with gratitude for your love and understanding.

Kristen Spexarth
August, 2015

Introduction

Passing Reflections Volume III: Surviving Suicide Loss Through Mindfulness is a chronological account of my journey of discovery through loss after my eldest son, Colby, died by suicide. Incorporated herein are selected poems from my book *Passing Reflections, Volume One: Meditations on Grief*, first published in 2002, and again with *Volume Two: The Journey Through Grief*, in 2010. Also included is a collection of more recent poems along with narrative introductions at the beginning of each section that give some context. The early poems came in a spontaneous and unbidden grief response while the narrative and later poems took years of mindfulness practice and thoughtful inquiry to articulate. The journal form has been maintained throughout to make it easier to follow the challenges I experienced as well as the growth that came over time.

It was difficult for me to find genuine help in the aftermath of trauma. Some people seemed to hesitate to reach out, perhaps because they could not bear to witness my pain. And, too, it is hard to connect with survivors like me whose lives have been torn asunder—the ground gives way, time stops, we cease to exist as once we did, almost as if there was no one there to reach. Especially hard was when people seemed to discount or deny my reality, unwilling to acknowledge something that was outside of their experience and theoretical comfort zone.

Traumatized, my body, heart and mind responded with physiological and mental processes that were of vital importance to my well-being. I had to enter this process to find healing but it was not an easy task and many recommended I avoid it, hoping that side-stepping difficulty would provide relief from my pain. I found the opposite to be true—to find relief I had to slowly and gently move toward the pain, gradually weaving loss into the fabric of my life in a way that I could manage.

In the beginning I felt profoundly alienated even from loving family and friends who were trying to help, even as I had an urgent need to connect with them in a meaningful way. I found myself inhabiting a parallel world, isolated in the midst of other's normalcy. It was frightening to be utterly transformed and apparently alone in a strange but vital new world.

As if dropped into a maze with no familiar feature or way to return to my used-to-be, the effects of trauma were bewildering. More than simply having unfamiliar features, the fundamental structure of the world appeared radically altered. My body seemed to lack hard edges and I felt more like a shockingly awake awareness in the midst of swirling energies. Finding a way to navigate my new environment became an urgent need. Just like Theseus in the labyrinth required the aid of a linen cord to the find his way back, for me writing and mindfulness meditation proved to be the lifelines that helped me through the labyrinth of traumatic loss. The sacred beauty of Puget Sound gave me respite and helped me find renewed strength to approach my grief work again and again. And counseling, both individual and group, were helpful.

The stress of being unable to communicate what was real for me set in motion the writing of this book. Desperately needing to connect with others and failing miserably in most of my attempts, I fell back on the written word. Deep in shock, at first my writing was simply witnessing, documenting where I was and what was happening inside of me. Later, as I experienced awkward and sometimes hurtful interactions with friends and caregivers, I wrote, trying to help people understand what it is to grieve deep loss.

After many years I have learned that while pain softens in time, it does not go away. Even so, through the slow process of mindful grieving my life has been profoundly enriched, a metamorphosis being the most apt description of my journey. The pain that once immobilized now energizes me to reach out to others suffering loss. This book documents my ongoing process of recovery. I offer it, hoping you will find herein threads of correspondence and the certainty that you are not alone for I believe this is where healing begins. While initially seeming impossible, I found a way to rebuild my life and I hope to create a bridge of understanding to help other trauma survivors, and anyone faced with difficulty, find a path of healing.

WHAT HAPPENED?

So complex is the unfolding of a life even seen in retrospect it is usually hard to discern where one path leaves off and another takes up, daily influences subtly shaping our growth and direction. But sometimes a single event can thrust one onto a path so divergent it could be likened to moving from two- to three-dimensional space. Once I was unaware of the magnitude of the epidemic raging through our communities even though the particulars of this scourge are commonplace and can be found in most local newspapers on a back page: another person ends life, a suicide. A numbing protects many of us from approaching these news clips with anything more than a casual glance or morbid curiosity. Those could never be our loved ones. Not ours. This book grew out of my life's dismantling and rebirth following the suicide of my eldest son, Colby, at the age of twenty-two.

As a child Colby had known prolonged periods of severe head pain from frequent ear infections and five surgeries for bilateral cholesteatoma over an eleven year span. Following the last surgery at sixteen his recovery was so swift it seemed his journey through pain was over but I was wrong. In the summer of his twentieth year he was stricken with head and neck pain initially triggered by a computer monitor at work. At first corrective glasses helped but the pain recurred and over the course of the next thirty months a succession of pain "triggers" progressively and inexorably narrowed his existence to a world were he could not look at computer screens or work, drive or go to movies, or look out windows, or use a glass cup, or read a book, or rollerblade, or be outside in the light of day, or take night walks on the beach, or listen to music, or write, or do any of the things that had once made his life so rich in love and activity.

In the spring of 1999, no longer able to live on his own, he came home. Colby saw numerous health professionals from a wide range of disciplines, alternative and traditional. Though his doctors never arrived at a clear diagnosis they kept trying, prescribing numerous drugs and therapies but nothing stopped the pain for more than a few hours at a time. Colby hurt so badly he could not lay his head down to sleep and had to prop himself in awkward positions that added to his extreme discomfort. Throughout this ordeal his girlfriend stayed close and I am certain that her loving presence helped him stay with us longer than he could otherwise have managed.

On the night of December 30, 2000, Colby checked into a motel and early the next morning put an end to the tormenting pain and with it his life, consequently ending my life as I knew it. I had never allowed myself to imagine his condition might be fatal. My attention was focused on finding the care he needed to get well. When the police walked darkly up our path with the grim news of Colby's death I was catapulted to a state of shock so deep I could barely breathe. All movement happened in very tentative slow motion as I struggled to simply drive to the store or make arrangements for the funeral home to receive his body or go to visit him there and hold his hand one last time. My family and friends came and without them I could not have managed. Soon after this my youngest son, Arlen, went back to college and I took time off from work, settling in for the long process of trying to comprehend what had happened.

Excerpts from Colby's Writing - 1998 — 2000

What a bloody mess, neh? Makes me think of the classic *Calvin and Hobbes* strip where Calvin, hanging from a helium balloon in the stratosphere, proclaims, "Life is never so bad it can't get worse." Seriously though, isn't the inverse also true? Never so good it can't get better? Bill Watterson, speaking for Calvin would say, "Possible, but worse is more likely." But then, what is worse? That's a concept directly related to our values in life. Values and ideals and perceptions which I can see are skewed in any one of a dozen possible scenarios, including the heaven/hell and Buddhist reincarnation "realities." What is important to you as a set of ideals is all that separates good and bad happenings. Place too much emphasis on things of passing notability and you'll be confronted with a life which is filled with "worse" or "worsening" situations. A change of perspective is then necessary, as most people do not enjoy dread (though some thrive in such areas). So what serves to delineate matters of perspective and true value. Or are all things subjective to better perspective enhancement? Simple question: What matters? (I didn't say it was an easier one). Is there a meta-standard by which things can be judged? In such a scenario what are the absolutes that dictate it? Religion offers some. And if you believe in a religion you have objects of absolute value, indifferent to perspective by definition. How fucking easy.

Maybe heaven weighed against hell is your absolute. Then it's pretty simple. "Questions on reality, kiddo? Visit your friendly Gideon for advice!" Or maybe you're pure empirical atheist. Then it would be, what, the torment of existence weighed against the horror of non-being? Not quite as simple, I think, but not a vast morass of inky unknown either. That little gem of a problem belongs to agnostics. Damn my neck hurts! Hay-zeus! Sheesh.

As I think about, as I see it, I'm smart. Of above average intelligence. I'm tall. Not bad looking, neither. I'm not burdened with abundant back hair. My feet have this amazing ability: they stay dry and cool all day long; never smell bad. I have not now, nor have I ever had any chemical dependencies or tendencies toward. My on the job work ethic is excellent, and will ensure my place up the corporate ladder, or so I have had the good fortune to be told by employers. My fingernails are resilient and don't break easily. I pick up skills well and am not hampered by psychological impediments to their improvement— plateauing has never been a problem. I'm also completely broken. Nine out of ten ain't bad.

When did I become broken and how did it occur? The former is simple enough: a sunny day in June 1998. The latter? Can't say for sure. I can say what I was doing at the time, how I felt, the shirt I was wearing and everything else I was in contact with physically. I can't tell you what happened. Nope. It was one of those ephemeral moments which is defining: A bomb dropped signals a war. The world at peace one fine afternoon, the next day's dawn a red haze of bloodshed. Sounds silly, but one morning I am thinking in terms of accomplishing a task that day to further myself toward my life goal: a puzzle piece of seven that comprise needed accomplishments for the week. In mind are the four larger blocks of seven comprising the month's efforts toward the life goal. The next morning I awake with a block of cement on my neck. Hanging there, heavily. A "stopping issue" in computer terms. The week's seven pieces crash to the ground, bringing the month's four with it. Three months and a promising abruptly ended career later, the year's intricate design hemorrhages into a coma.

Have you ever tasted defeat? I haven't. But I have tasted paradise, on a walk filled with sweat and planning and hardship. A paradise of my dreams, of my own making. It seemed deserved. It felt real. Something to give reason to hurt, tears, blood. I taste it in dreams now and its flavor fills my days with horror. A wrenching, ironically, not achievable without once bathing in its warm taste. A drug whose withdrawal is infinite and never lessening. To walk there but for a day or a week and cling to its essence makes suffering almost worth it.

Plans, and with them hopes collapse under their no longer supported weight. Taking with them the puzzle pieces of sweat used to prop them in the first place.

Bleeding. Slowing. Faltering. Fight so hard with so much to fight for, I raise my machete to the concrete wall again and again. Swing hard swing fast. But I know I'm bleeding. I swing my blade at the wall, willing the concrete to yield before me. Pounding, sweat dripping off my forehead. Someone passes by and hands me a new machete, pats me on the back.

Swinging, fighting, smashing. Bleeding.

Doctors are not healers. Do not mistake them for such. Only the body heals, and it only heals itself. Doctors clear impediments to the body's healing, impediments it cannot handle itself. They do a great service helping the body help itself, but they are healer's aides at best. And they are not always aides. Hope heals. Hope fights. It is part of the body, it is healer. Doctors who inhibit, retard, or fail to promote hope are not doctors. They are not healer's aides. They are parasites of the body's energy. Lessening its ability to fight for itself. Beware the doctor who carries the invisible lancet.

Light at the end of the tunnel. You can see it. Within reach. The end. But how far? How long? I will walk until I can walk no more. Indeed. I will ignore my thirst and my pain. All it takes is a little time. Walk. More. Is the light getting brighter? Indeed. Getting sleepy now. But it's there. Traveled so far for it, worked so hard to get there. But I'm almost there. Indeed. My feet are heavy, but I'll drag them. Was I thirsty? Can't feel my throat. Is that the light? I can barely make it out. Not much further. Indeed. So tired now. I can move if I crawl. Maybe I'll just rest here. Yes, so good to rest. I'll be able to move once I sleep. Oh, there's the light. It was much closer than I thought. Indeed.

Welcome to my day. Welcome to purgatory. I feel a great weight on my forehead, like a palm pressing down, forcing. It hurts more on the left than the right. The muscles around my left eye are tight and squeezing, distorting my vision. A tight grasping pressure grips my throat, mostly on the left. It presses into my throat, distorting, ever so slightly, my voice. Making speech more difficult. At the back of my neck, base of the skull, in the occipital region and on the left is a great, dull pain. The right side is unaffected. The pain on the left is akin to a thumb being forced into the area at maximum pressure. Massively painful. It never stops, not nightly nor randomly. Taken together, these areas are what I would rate a seven on a ten scale of pain and I obsess about them. They don't leave me ever. I am constantly aware of them. Triggers such as monitors (CRT & LCD) drive pain to nine. Mini-migraines with visual aura come and go many times weekly, bringing pain to nine of ten. Classic migraine symptoms. God help me.

Purgatory. A place of waiting. Not moving forward nor backward. Not life, but death neither. Punishment? Depends on who you ask. A place of reflection, remorse for things missed or futures imagined. Frustration. A crucible with a view of mistakes made and a prison of impotence of the now. Burning as I wait. Twisting as I watch. Hating, Hating, Hating. I can see the flowers grow and bloom from my box, my crucible. I watch them flourish under the sun and bask in life. Rain mists leaves making them more beautiful. The flowers, so vibrant, so fragile. They press knives to my flesh and carve, smiling, their bladed happiness. With only my crucible to keep me warm, burning me alive. Purgatory. Where is the end? When have I suffered enough? What exactly did I do for this?

The measure of a man is not how he stands in times of comfort and convenience, but how he stands in times of challenge and controversy.

— MLK

They say pain reminds you you're alive. And more pain reinforces this knowledge. More pain teaches appreciation of life without it. More pain educates you how selfishly others live without it. Still more, reveals fallacies in perceptions of life, shows shortcomings of human understanding. Immerse yourself in it and you will find mysteries solved and other mysteries posed. Breathe pain, breathe it and walk with it beside you until you cannot see where you stop and it begins. Here, in this place of joining will you see a truth. And in this truth is but one thing.

> *Did I request thee, maker, from my clay to mould me*
> *man? Did I solicit thee from darkness to promote me?"*
>
> — *Paradise Lost*

I am pathetic.
I am a broken fool with ridiculous hopes.
I am weak. I cannot handle pain.
I am shattered flesh which should be evolved right out of the gene pool for my weakness.
I am stupid and have failed to save myself because I am unintelligent.
I crumble at the first sign of hardship.
I am a worthless asshole.
I am weak.
I leech off of others to compensate for my inadequacy.
I convince myself I am doing a good job to ease my lazy conscience and rationalize my sub-marginality.
I am pedantic and berate others with strength.

But

I have survived 18 months of pain of immense magnitude.
I have struggled to save myself by seeing thirty-eight doctors.
I have lasted through 200 appointments.
I have endured disbelief, belittling, and indifference.
I have lost independence, career, friends.
I have seen the secret of life.

I try.

THE DREAM
FROM SPRING OR SUMMER 2000

I'm on the side of a mountain, sitting on a rock above a small flat area. In the area right below me is a surveyor's sighting tool mounted in stone facing a stone building. The building is about 10' high, 10' wide and 20' deep, has no windows or doors. The surveying telescope thing points toward its wall and is about 5 feet away from it. Since it is mounted in stone it is immobile. I spend a lot of time here on the rock above this area. People come and look through the sight and marvel, then leave. Some study what they see for a long time before they leave. They talk among themselves about it, wondering. They leave disappointed but not sad that they couldn't solve its mystery.

Looking through the site one sees the interior of the building with no windows. The inside is brightly lit and devoid of anything—no chairs, pictures, it's an empty room. On the far wall there is a tile about 3/4 the way up the wall. It has a simple design on it. It is cockeyed to the left, turned out of position from the wall. Its being out of position is very wrong. Right behind it on the wall is its "socket" where it would fit in if it were turned back to its rightful angle. Everyone who looks into the room through the site wishes they could get into the room to turn the tile back into place, but no one knows how to get into the room. I'm both angry and disgusted at these people, though not visibly. They look through the site, think about it, take notes, confer, then leave. Time passes. Much time. Then one day I climb down from the rock again to look through the site. Someone nice is on my left, helping me with good ideas. I can't see who, I don't look over, I know they're nice. Looking through the site I suddenly realize everyone has been going about this wrong. Thinking about it wrong.

They've been looking at it the wrong way! They should have been looking through the site from the opposite side. As soon as I realize this I am inside the room with my back to the tile. I can see people outside looking through the site—the wrong way still—and seeing me inside the room. Their expressions are that of wonderment. I know what to do now. I turn and approach the tile slowly. I look at the tile up close, at its simple design. I reach up and twist it back into place. It sinks back into the wall with a *click* perfect fit. Immediately I leave my body. It ceases to exist. I am filled with joy and ecstasy to no limit. No longer physical, my mind expands and flies from the room. I have transcended my humanity and am something else now. I look back at the people still looking through the site with a sense of pity. Even if they knew how they were doing it wrong they could not achieve this, I am certain. I now have boundless energy and no physical constraints. My consciousness, full of joy, floats over the mountain. I wake up.

COLBY'S DREAM
FROM MAY 19, 2000

dictated to me since he could no longer write

Colby is standing in front of 1519 (his childhood home). There's a green lawn and standing there someone comes up to him with a big grin on and says "They're coming," and leaves. He was a man—tall white guy who was a friend of his. He said "They're coming for you," he left.

There was a wave of people walking first. Then guys on Harleys. Then more and more people. It was an unending parade. Maybe ten thousand people came by. All in groups:

Walking, motorcycles, biking, pushing a stroller, running, walking sideways—can't remember. About the same number per group, no difference.

They didn't look at him—they were doing the parade—and Colby was the only person there. Some would wave and smile but not at him. It felt like it was a massive, grandiose epic. Felt like an event, not a dream. It was for Colby...It has some significance he didn't understand.

When he awoke he felt he hadn't slept, but been involved in this event the whole time. It wasn't so much a dream, it was an event. There were also maybe one or two people next to him and behind him. Can't see them, he just knew they were there. One on each side. They felt familiar. The people in the parade he'd never met, didn't know them at all.

To sum it up would be to belittle it, no particular theme, it just is.

The dream was so mundane but when he woke up he didn't think it was a dream. It felt really good. Felt huge. It was a big deal.

Colby's Last Note
found January 7, 2001

on four pages in the center of a blank book in his closet, tucked amidst his Calvin and Hobbes *collection*

I find myself out of time before my time. Unfortunate, but it cannot be helped. I've done all I can do now. It was a ton of fun, and if I could do it all again...Well, I wouldn't change much. I have no real regrets. Why did I pick up this pen? What do I have to say? Life is so beautiful, in its triumphs and tragedies. Everywhere I look I see it now. There is beauty even in fear and pain, but visible only to those deeply submerged in it. I have exhausted myself physically and emotionally. My pain is now breathtakingly acute and intense. I fear a continued downward slide to where I no longer have the ability to free myself. I do not accept life in this condition, as is my right. It is both undignified and unpleasant. I have eliminated all possibility of a medical solution, visiting 40+ doctors for over 150 visits combined and attempted dozens of treatments. My condition, which has a definite and predictable pathology, may not be terminal. In its cruelty, however, it may as well be. I am not clinically depressed and have been confirmed in this belief by numerous psychologists and one psychiatrist. Perhaps that is why the next step is so difficult for me, though I desire it. I have loved and been loved in life and been blessed in more ways than I could have asked. Beauty and love. It is so very painful physically now even to write this, so I'll sum up my major points. Sheer pain. Increasing dramatically these days. My current existence is undignified and a burden to my family. I have learned more in 22 years than many will in their lifetimes.

Peace, love, and don't forget to floss daily.

Love,
Colby
[Sometime in 2000]

P.S. Automatic transmissions are for wusses only!

Book One

January 2001

Traveling the road of recovery after trauma is an arduous task. In the beginning there was only the sense of space and a flow of energy, as if there were no familiar edges to my body. Feeling alone and confused, I tried to find my way slowly and clumsily, one step at a time. My senses were heightened such that I could viscerally feel people's energy as they approached. When they came with fear, as often happened, their energy hit me with a force almost like being kicked in the stomach. I had to retreat from being with people who meant to help but whose aversion created further difficulty.

Fear causes us to tighten, trying to put up barriers hoping to protect ourselves. Now, there was nothing left to protect. Returning to a familiar "normal" to help others feel safe in an uncertain world was impossible. As frightening as it was to feel alone in my new reality, it was even more frightening to contemplate return to the shadow-like wasteland of surface living, the so-called comfort zone where some choose to exist trying to keep their fears at bay.

The trauma of my son's death opened me to a new way of being. My former world and almost everything that had once been meaningful to me was obliterated. While the unfamiliar feelings and sensations coursing through my body were exhausting and strange, also present was a vitality and clarity that I needed to explore.

I understood now that trying to barricade myself hoping to stave off fear doesn't work. When Colby told me he could not go on if the pain continued I went into hyperdrive, on the one hand searching for help while on the other, sinking into denial unable to acknowledge my fear of losing him. Now I saw that trying to keep a lid on things by stuffing fear is much like an ostrich putting its head in the sand. Changes come that force us to grow no matter how much we try to keep things "safe" and the same.

My supervisor helped me patch together time off from work and feeling utterly lost, I went to Idaho for a week to lend a hand to my brother and sister-in-law after her surgery. Having kept a journal for years it was natural for me to record what was happening, finding myself in a parallel world where I could not reach out to others nor could they reach in to me.

TALONS

It's winter in northern Idaho and every other day or so snow squalls completely obscure the view from my brother's living room, white-out erasing the bay. This landscape shrouded in snow, even the sun shines silvery cold. So stark is the beauty here but not cruel. That would be a sentimental overlay on something that needs no embellishment. I sit and watch coots swimming in great flocks, thousands strong. Resembling an amoeba, the whole constantly changes shape, elongating and coalescing within invisible boundaries. Individuals glide sometimes with, sometimes against the current, responding to a subtle unseen order. Diving randomly, practicing survival skills, waterspouts appear

suddenly here and there within the body of the flock.
When eagles come the coots tighten into a knot of
explosive water. One eagle hovers and dives over and
over trying for the flock separated coot. One might
think the odds favor eagles but I'm told it isn't necessarily
so. Despite their strength, one-on-one duels are often
lost to sheer exhaustion. Today, the familiar drama
continuing nearby, the amoeba relaxes a bit and swims
slowly away. Every time the long submerged coot
resurfaces the eagle is right there hovering, reaching and
zip! Down goes the coot again and again. Suspended,
constantly dancing on water the eagle appears to tire.
Indeed, it gives up on the one and soars over the flock
scattering it in waves of panic like soap on an oil slick.
My sister-in-law tells me this eagle seems a new
breed. Abandoning the usual it dives into the group,
plunging into the mass, grabbing for anything its talons
might find. Several times it dives either in a desperate
attempt or perhaps a brilliant new strategy. The coots
disassemble themselves, undone. Quiet comes, the flock
settling down restored next to a dark blob on the water.
Straining to see what is happening I imagine the eagle
has drowned. But no, a head lifts, then back down again
an ink spot until finally it raises itself high enough to
gain purchase on the waves and begins to move toward
shore. Huge wings extend pulling at the water, over and
over, covering the hundred feet or so between the kill and
solid ground. Awe struck I watch transfixed. Emerging
from the lake, slowly dragging itself and prey up at the
fish hatchery boat ramp, the eagle tears into the drowned
coot and feeds.

The next day I saw three eagles working a duck. Though resembling a coot there was no flock in the bay and they travel in a crowd. This one had to be a bufflehead, the female mostly black like a coot with a little white spot on the side of her head, now hidden. Her constant companion was nowhere to be seen. The eagles took turns hovering and diving as the bufflehead dove and dove and dove and dove. Only one conceivable end to this struggle the odds being what they were. I put down the field glasses and turned away, back to my own breakfast of oatmeal and summer frozen raspberries.

Later that day I went for a walk. Was encouraged to do so in fact, probably in hopes I might air my head out a bit from the intensity of helping with my sister-in-law's recovery. She was so sick we had slept little all week. That and grieving the sudden and desperate death of my eldest son had washed me out. After years of struggling and enduring, pried open by pain he simply found the strength to end. From my newly found vantage I discerned encouragement, loving but firm, to try another point of view. Didn't especially want to go out. I was content sitting on my perch when I wasn't helping as if I were the eagle surveying her domain. Couldn't even imagine moving so much was happening inside me; energy spinning in my center and tears coming in fierce waves as my mind wandered trying to gather up the pieces of lives torn asunder.

I went and stood outside on the deck, stared across the yard, across the bay and realized I didn't know what to do. From the deck the sandy shoreline was invisible. Starting down the stairs crusted over ice I set out toward the beach where the snow, maybe eighteen inches deep, stopped abruptly at water's edge. My boots crunching and sinking up to my calves, I decided to walk along the shore where the going would be easier. Good, tall, black rubber boots made it possible to walk in the water, actually in the waves, so I made my way walking aimlessly looking at my slow feet being washed by the waves and the pebbles time tumbling into sand. Nowhere to go, just going, I headed south toward the fish hatchery. Crossed alternately over and under the docks mostly high and dry now with the lowering of the lake level in winter. The one where the muskrats live was partly under water. I looked and could see gathered straw and a narrow hole that went down at an angle. What a pleasure viewing from aloft the antics of that pair, looking everything like little pieces of driftwood floating upwind until they reanimated and dove.

The day was cold and clear, icy blue canopy and a fresh dusting of snow on the forest covering the surrounding hills except where the shore houses carved out space. No wind to speak of, the gentle waves were barely ruffled by the breeze. Traveling one foot in front of the other most of my surroundings were lost on me until I came upon a curiosity: a rusted out truck engine in the lake, winter exposed a few yards from the water's edge. Pondering the "why" of a full-sized truck engine in a lake I turned to see where I was. Then I saw.

Knew right away I'd stumbled upon the last of the bufflehead who had struggled and lost her life that morning. Glancing over my shoulder and gauging the distance to the house confirmed my suspicions. Closer

7

I saw a disturbed area ten feet wide. Two blood spots staining the new snow and the deep print of one huge eagle talon surprised me. But most amazing was the pattern of wings on each side maybe eight feet apart where giant feathers had swept the snow then propped the eagle as it fed. Each stroke was clearly laid down, a dance frozen in time. Circling this were dog tracks and then another circle outside that, my own trail as I skirted the site trying to fully understand. We who happened by here did not disturb the place itself, respectfully witnessing, and the snow scribe made it easy to read the record.

I turned back to the house once again walking in the water on the edge between two worlds. Thought to myself: "Life is not cruel, it just is." Even if we search forever, trying to gather the why of things or fathom the depths of a human heart cannot bring us to a place of knowing. My son is gone like the coot, the bufflehead and magnificent tracks in snow. All now part of me and everything. Back at the house I made a new fire. Churning center, I sat on my crag by the window learning how to open to a heart torn wide by love's talons.

January 2001
Sandpoint

ONCE IN A WHILE

Once in a while
we notice each other
and noticing,
reach out.

Once in a while
we get quiet enough
to touch the pain.

Once in a while
a stranger's kindness
stops me in my tracks
long enough
to finally see where I am,
spinning in oblivion.

January 2001
Sandpoint

REFLECTIONS

Reflections press in upon me
closer and closer,
everywhere I look,
layer upon layer
builds to a crushing load.

When the break comes
all goes crashing down.
The contents of a life,
my life,
your life,
scattered randomly.

Not even enough energy
to look for the pieces.
Empty now.
Still.

January 2001
Sandpoint

Paradox

How could we have done it differently?
Such a silly question
after the fact.
So much seems clear now and yet,
even the puzzle pieces coming together
do not reveal your heart
so well concealed, so methodical.
I took your signals
to be signs of recovery,
holiday spirits high
gaming with the family
all smiles for us, renewed.
If you were calling out for help,
no one could hear you,
the time for help long past in your eyes.
In control, master of your fate,
alone.
Besides the pain which was enough
you felt you were a burden.
You did not understand!
Until chained and bound by love
we cannot know freedom.
My life found meaning
within those constraints
the paradox revealed.
Still, grown to a man
the choice was yours
alone.

January 2001
Seattle

Waiting Room

What is it about hospital floors
the corridors so polished and long?
Sitting any length of time
I get to watch shadows of passing strangers
approach and depart.
Sitting in the funeral home
no one at the front desk
alone in the quiet
of that large, sunny front room
tastefully decorated with photos
of loving scenes filled
with people,
forced to still myself
waiting
on your ashes
the hollow urgency gnawing
at my belly, sweeping through,
emptying me.
Only the flow of energy now
pressing through my center.
Then I see the flickering
lights passing across
the high walls right in front of me.
Coming. Going.
Sunlight bouncing off passing cars
like the aura of a migraine dancing.
Light passing across the halls of death
crossing over.

January 2001
Seattle

February 2001

It took all my strength to simply sit with the energy that was coursing through my body unlike anything I'd ever known. In shock, I struggled to come to terms with incidents that happened on the night Colby died.

Following an argument on the evening of December 30th I'd left the house, very upset, and went for a walk. On returning, I saw that Colby was in the garage, preparing to drive away, so I went inside not wanting to confront him. At that moment I had a dissociative experience, where I saw my body walk away and could not turn it around, even though my awareness was struggling to bring it back. Words came, "You will regret this, you need to acknowledge him," and still I could not manage to unite body and witness. Suddenly, I was up the stairs in the kitchen, whole again, when I heard his car start. I ran to the front door and out on the walk where he would have to drive past me to leave when it happened again. Frustrated, unable to direct the movement of my body as it walked toward the house, I heard again, "You will regret," and then found myself inside the house, body and awareness reunited, watching Colby drive away. To this day I am mystified by these events.

Around two in the morning, after hours of fretful worry followed by a sleepy miscommunication with his brother, I mistakenly thought both my sons were home. Relieved that they were safe I headed to bed. As I lay down a sphere of light came through my window almost as if the moon entered the room, turned a right angle toward me and then entered my forehead. Immediately, I was simply awareness without a body in a place that was lit with radiant yet soft white light, with a sense of spacial depth but empty of any feature. Beyond all descriptions that words can offer I felt at peace and knew, "Colby's safe!" I heard, "There is nothing wrong and there has never been anything wrong," and then I slept.

I have no referent to help me understand this experience or how long it lasted. Upon waking I went about my morning, making lists, happy for the holiday weekend ahead. Unlike other times when I've had curious experiences, this time I did not think to myself, "What was that?" Even when the police arrived later that morning with news of Colby's death, the experience of luminous and blissful emptiness from the night before was not part of my thought process. Later, when learning of the approximate time of his death it occurred to me that the light that came to me that night was the essence of my son, sharing with me an experience of ultimate peace.

Even though I have no rational way to explain this, a "knowing" arrived with the experience of light that has lived inside of me since the moment it occurred, is part of my very being and has helped me to weather the worst of my grieving process. Paradoxically, I knew with every cell of my body that nothing was wrong while, in fact, everything was desperately wrong! Colby was gone, dead at twenty-two by his own hand. The tension between an experience of indescribable peace on the one hand and inconceivable pain on the other fueled the writing of the poems and essays that follow. After a month I went back to work but the gulf separating me from all but a few close family and friends seemed to grow wider. Some people's attempts at interaction were so unfeeling I ceased all contact. Meanwhile, I could pass for normal, working and speaking when spoken to but those closest to me knew I was barely present. A shadow, living in what appeared to be a shadowland where few real communications took place, I wrote whenever I could, trying to document and understand my new world.

On Colby's birthday I took the day off work wanting to honor him, desperate to find some equilibrium. At home, reading over words written since his death I saw movement in the work and thought it might be helpful to note the time and place of each poem. Similar to the journals I've kept for years, I imagined some thread of meaning might emerge over time. At this point I began to add the date and place for each poem and from that vantage, recalled the place and approximate time of the poems that had come prior to February 16.

The Cats are Mystified

My cats used to scramble
pell mell,
paws skittering
in their haste
to make way
such a rush I lived!
Barely starting one thing
I'd be butterfly on to the next
scattering cats before me.

Now they sit curled
slumping into me
deep trust,
liquid gaze,
sleepily wondering.
my movements
stilled.

Inside something is afoot.
Intense energy flowing,
quieting.
Your death,
riveting me to this couch,
has opened a door.

February 2001
Seattle

WHAT IS WRONG
WITH THIS PHONE?

Friends from afar wonder
how to approach
this abyss,
try to reach out
to hold me
but I cannot be reached.

How, I don't know,
but a few make it through.
The ones who sit simply
going nowhere,
nothing to say,
fearless,
quietly witness the whirlwind
passing through.

February 2001
Seattle

Inconceivable

Have you ever noticed
we cannot see anything
till our minds conceive
it possible?
Mostly we muddle
through impressions and imaginings
gazing out at life with dim awareness
as through smoke of new fire,
poor draft, fuel obscured,
never realizing it is we
who will burn.
For me your leaving was inconceivable.
Bound by perceptions
filled with myself
I missed you
making preparations.

Past all reckoning,
crucible of your days
burning,
you came to the place
nothing mattered but release.
I heard you
rage spewing, hurt full,
thought your words aimed
to strike me
not cut the bonds, a mother's claim
that held you.
Driven by forces beyond fathoming
you readied yourself, alone.

Something in me saw your leaving,
knew this was not simple argument
as I watched
strangeness of myself
somehow separate from body,
auto pilot walking away,
unable to give acknowledgement
even as the watcher longing to reach for you
said, "You will regret."

Seven days and four pages later
there it was
in the center of a blank book
I gave to you for dreaming.
Could tell your hand,
knew what I'd found to be the missing note
months old now I guessed
reaching us across the divide.
Now, fire inside, illusion burning,
unable to move, I see.
Blinded to your reality
fearing loss I lived in dream
unable to conceive your end.
Crucified by pain
you did the only thing you could.

The night you died you came to me,
yellow ball of light, white rays circling round,
suddenly in front of then into me.
Words rose, instantaneous relief,
"Colby's safe!" then sleep.
Through eyes open or closed
I don't even know

I finally saw you, light
evaporating fear.
Now I ponder and cannot grasp thinking
what is already clear.
So I bounce between tangled pain
of loss beyond counting
and certainly that I suffer from suffering,
unnecessary construct, habit of this living.

There is about life a numbing, veil donning
that takes and muddies certain knowing
but true sight, if only a glimmer
and once in a lifetime
leaves a subtle, unseen, indelible print.
Peace beyond knowing
inconceivable after all
seen even once changes everything.

February 2001
Seattle

THE LUMPERS AND THE SPLITTERS TRY TO DECIDE WHAT'S REAL

After a lifetime spent
trying to put things together
in my mind
studying, labeling,
discerning, qualifying,
separating every twig from branch,
tree from tree,
personality from personality,
holding my eldest son's
ashes
in this small,
six-sided, black receptacle
wrapped in white paper
finally I see.
There is no way
he could ever fit in this box
or any of the boxes
I ever made for him.
Luminous and empty
he is everything
and everywhere
showing me the way to my heart
to be at peace with multiplicity
while seeking the origins.

February 16, 2001
Seattle

THE LUMPERS AND THE SPLITTERS TRY TO GET ALONG AT WORK

I understand your intentions are managerial.
We are dissonant personalities
with contrary predilections.
Hoping to find a way
to emulsify our thinking
you try to unmask the essence
of each
but as your further split
or variously gather us together
into well researched,
tidy
and static boxes
with labels of "feeling" or "rational"
from which each can clearly view the other,
can't you see the distances
growing?
The judgments
cementing themselves
into righteous corners of habituation?
It is true understanding you seek?
That would blow all the boxes away
laying waste to the lumping
and the splitting
as we suddenly knew ourselves
to be the other.
Let's stop this nonsense
and start our practices
in earnest.

February 16, 2001
Seattle

EARLY ON

I tried
but could not find you,
your scent, on the laundry you left
crumpled in the basket in your closet.
I meant to bury myself in it,
to draw you in
but could find no trace.
Now, forth-nine days have passed
since your death.
Took the laundry to wash
to finally let go
trying to honor you by not clinging,
to help you find your way
through what I imagined
were layers of confusion
and fear.
Separating light
from dark
there you were in your white tee
with the collar cut out
to ease the pain
not to chafe or bind at all.
I could not wash it.
Two days later I picked you up
in your tee
and drank you in
one last time.
Smelling you there
bent me in half
to feel what I have lost.

Begging your forgiveness
for my clinging
the only words I can find
are "ok, ok, ok,"
my mantra nowadays
as I struggle to find
passage through my confusion
and fear.

February 17, 2001
Seattle

TIDE AND WIND

Tears upon tears
who opened these floodgates?
There is no stemming this tide
as it washes over me,
washing me away.

People call.
I hear fear in the voices
but there is nothing to fear,
the worst already done.

The anchor of your living here
gone
the winds of my soul
are drifting
aimlessly.

February 18, 2001
Seattle

Sunflowers on Blue

You put them there
months ago.
Helping me
set up my computer
you found a site
where beautiful scenes
scroll through my screen
randomly.

Sunflowers!
I reach up to touch them
as if
touching them
I could reach you
randomly.

February 19, 2001
Seattle

DAY 55

Today was the first in quite a while
that I could listen to the CDs,
the ones you burned of all my favorite songs
gifted to me for Christmas.
Before this I had patience only
to listen to chanting prayer
and the sound of my own voice
reading Tibetan wisdom;
help for the living, the dying,
the dead.
The act of doing something,
anything,
that might in fact be of service to your soul
trying to help you helped me.
You asked for the titles repeatedly.
I was so busy!
Heard your eagerness to be excitement
to share your great skill
gift of yourself
I thought always available.
After all, you, my eldest,
along with your brother
I wore on my arms like jewels.
Your name even said it,
"Colby, from the coal town," the book read
but I saw instead human being building,
squeezing, transforming,
trusted life forces working
on blessed and beloved child.
So I chose in your naming,
"coal into diamond,"
my dreams for you were so large.

27

How could I know the gifted metaphor
would be so apt?
You, flesh and blood, not stone,
never meant to carry the life load given you
in the crushing that came,
the pain that was yours throughout.
And your gift to me?
I hurriedly handed you song list of a lifetime
and you, CDs covered in roses,
ended the giving by dying.
Or so I thought but see now there's more
since your giving has kept on opening doors
teaching me essence unending
beyond all imagining,
light filled and love full,
guiding me still.

February 23, 2001
Seattle

THE GIFTS

Somehow
to say
only
and all
that I know
to be true.
Never to fear
anything,
least of all
judgment,
my own
or others.'
These are
the gifts
you have given me
in death
and in them
you have gifted me
life.

February 24, 2001
Seattle

Cocoon

Such an odd feeling,
edges of my body
indistinct,
center empty of content
and yet somehow full,
energy radiating.
Breath comes
in shallow drafts
panting
as if giving birth.
I sit and spin
this intangible cocoon
never quite knowing
if I'm mending the rend
in my soul
or unraveling my tether
to solid form.
The fullness is
not hungry, wants
no companionship.
Everything outside of this
I do as if in dream
the heart of me elsewhere spinning
a web connecting to
another place.

February 25, 2001
Seattle

Cat Cushion

Completely useless
this saving of things,
stashing and hoarding
and putting away
for the future.
You are gone and I
never gave you the book
with all my observations
of your youth!
Never pulled from the lockbox
the dollar bill
the nurse gave you
on the day your were born.
A gift of apology
because you were made to wait.
Of what use now that you are gone?
Indeed, of what use am I now
save as cat cushion?
They come to me as I lie
watching the fire,
on my chest, on my legs,
on the floor nearby.
Sufficient softness,
warmth and girth.
Nearly motionless
I am perfect for this work.

March 2001

In years past I harbored the illusion that I could direct the course of my life by the power of my will alone. I carried this notion, putting pressure on myself hoping to create imagined outcomes. This strategy seemed to work until challenges came that were too large for me to untangle, too complex to fully comprehend. While Colby, his doctors and I were all confounded by his mysterious illness still I struggled to manage things as I had always done, wasting myself with worry, searching for something that would help, as he tried every treatment we could find to alleviate his pain. Hoping to create a desired outcome our combined efforts, which seemed Herculean to me, were to no avail.

Sometimes trying harder doesn't help. Some barriers do not give way no matter how much effort we expend to overcome them. Pain clinics offer techniques to help one live with pain but Colby was not interested in working with his pain, he wanted it to go away. Having witnessed my son's suffering, I felt tremendous loss but no anger at him. I could not judge his action as right or wrong, it was simply the best he could do under extreme circumstances.

What aroused my anger was the response some people gave me when learning of his death, people who had no idea what he had been going through or how fiercely he had struggled to survive. Their responses were simply a knee-jerk reaction, judgements that arose from fear, which I understood since once upon a time I had done the same.

Paradoxically, the trauma of losing Colby tore away the blinders that previously hindered my vision. Trauma taught me that my efforts to control were misguided. The challenges that come offer us the opportunity to grow and when the challenges are great, to be transformed. Now I understood that life moves through us, shaping us in ways that are impossible to imagine at the outset. In that process we have a choice: allow life to move through us freely or resist the changes and the challenges that come. Judgements represent resistance, imagining there is an ideal that we must meet that is different from what IS.

What I learned through traumatic loss is a simple fact— the only aspect of life we can control is our response to whatever comes to us. This is not an easy lesson to absorb and one person's answer will be different from another's. Trauma catapulted me past concepts of "right" and "wrong" to an understanding that life is larger than I ever imagined and could not be contained in any judgments I, or anyone else, might offer. Beyond concepts, the fact of Colby's death was something I needed to learn to live with if I was going to survive.

THE LONGING

Needing to fill inner void
wanting from other
what cannot be given
looking for the key, grasping,
we struggle to find a way
out of loneliness and fear.
Hurtling through days giddy
pace, desperate
accumulating, lifetime's
longing drives us
to ever greater lengths.
Directionless we dig ourselves in deeper
with each pass.
Distractions bursting relationships launched
in frantic lethargy
across our foreheads messages we see.
What is this nuance
shining through pentimento,
leaf print on rock,
reflection on pane of glass?
After fruitless trying
broken, dying, something tells me,
"Trust the longing, bring it home."
No need for locks or security
hearts opening to luminosity.

March 3, 2001
Seattle

HIGH WATER

Don't mind me
if while we're talking
the tears come pouring down.
My already high water table
is overflowing the banks
of my being,
the climate so altered
since you've gone.
El Niño is back.
If it weren't for these tears
we'd have no rain at all.

March 7, 2001
Seattle

PRIMITIVE EVOLVING

Twenty-three years
and eons ago
I rested in delusion
thinking some escape suffering.
I would sit
not in judgment
and with good intentions
separate
making sure there was
comfortable distance
between myself
and other.
Primordial fear
seeping through
kind smiles,
touching trouble
might infect,
contagion wildfire spreading.
I kept myself
aloof from hard
dis-ease of any kind
hoping to be spared
a life of pain.
Relaxing into soft
clothed and fed
housed happily
partnered, child full and prideful,
looking back over my shoulder,
seeming grace full
and grateful to be
not you
I pictured the other shoe

dropping elsewhere.
Even told my friend,
trauma toppled,
"Won't let you go down,"
word salve to ease
our discomfort
I hoped would be enough.

Deep down I knew better.
Saw cracks in dreaming
crumble foundation
build blind.
Eventually, lifetimes later
I embraced the hard
lessons to be learned
awareness dawning
grace realized.
Saw as I drew you closer
resemblance.
Now this, my son's suicide,
life's pain personified
gift of awakening
has finally closed the gap.
Me and you
now one
all fear has fled.
I sit merged in new awareness
seeing others pass
looking over their shoulders
at me.

March 10, 2001
Seattle

A MOTHER'S LAMENT

If I could take you in my arms
and hold you
I would do so now.
How could I not feel attachment?
You, first born fruit
of my body's seed
glorious and beautiful son.
I loved you more than the sun,
the moon
and stars into infinity.
Now sirens sounds scream for my attention.
I'll say to myself
as I once read to you,
"Do not be distracted,
do not be afraid,"
this world and everything
mirrors of mind imagining.
Life,
death,
there is no separation.
Releasing form
my love for you
(or is it you?)
stays near comforting.

March 10, 2001
Seattle

Broken Hearted — Day 71

Shock filled
at first the grieving was all emptiness
absence of feeling.
Now the pain comes tripping
falling hurt over soft songs you favored.
Everything a barrier,
simply by your absence
I cannot seem to move through this space.
It lingers and fills my days.
So hard, a child dead before
and by his own hand!
My horror at this returns to haunt me daily.
Comfort is yours now
beyond pain, safe at last
released.
But me, I am lost in this living without you.
Broken hearted, swamped
by soggy marsh of tears
searching for a message
trusted life lesson
tell myself to do one thing, every day
to honor you and celebrate life.
Struggling to manage this
feel like simply fading away.
I thought birthing was hard.
Burying you may be more than I can do.

March 11, 2001
Seattle

SPUR

Hoping to comfort
friends quantify grieving
say, "Thirteen months,
That's how long it takes, on average,
to leave one layer of loss."
I know they mean well, wish me ease,
so I listen, respecting
knowing they, too, have grieved.
To me it matters little how long it takes.
I'm in no hurry.
Carried you nine months inside
and five years in my arms.
Around my neck and waist
arms, legs, limpet clinging,
you rode on my back till seven or eight.
Ferrying you and your brother
we rode out the years
team of three continually.
Even as you broke free
finding sweet life on your own,
handsome, strong, kind man that you were
still I carried you in thoughts
prized, and prize of my loving.
Pain is, but not the biggest part
along with your memory here in my heart
and it's welcome, a reminder,
like spur in soft flesh says, "Sleeper awake!
You have work to do yet."

March 17, 2001
Seattle

The Weight

Irreality of these days catches me off guard.
Every now and then life feels almost normal
and looking up I think,
"Can he really be gone? So much is the same,"
but that's wrong.
Simply by your absence all is askew.
Waking bereft, stomach pitted,
I realize I cannot go on
somnambulist creature habit trails caged.
I have yet to learn how to fit myself
around the immense hole you have torn
in the fabric of my life.
The weight on my chest never leaves,
makes breathing an effort as if
a great stone bound sigh rested there.
Not pain like yours 24-7, just watchful presence
deliberate and slow, large ungainly animal
lumbering heavily through minefield.
Trying to do simple tasks soon find myself stretched
over chasm of exhaustion barely clinging to sides
kite ready to fly with the slightest breeze.
A trip to the grocery becomes epic
undertaking, tentatively done.
Some watching this dance think me odd.
But you who have lost a piece of yourself
that made sense of living, recognize, nod,
conspiracy of silence
restraining scream.

March 22, 2001
Seattle

Rules In 3-D

In some circles
there are rules to this living
that must be kept for fear.
Holding the fact that you died, suicide,
to myself is quite clearly included.
The 3-Ds: death, divorce, disease
are not to be discussed.
Must not pop bubble of living
balanced so precariously
their mention might topple the timid.
"Don't get near me!" she cried, terrified,
when three of four PTA mothers
sitting bake sale together
shared news of impending divorces
and she wasn't kidding.
Fearing contagion of spirit
that might cause introspection
perhaps leading to loss
of kept house and views,
better to close the blinds.
Also remember,
tears are especially rude
invading calm, spreading pain
so few want to touch or take in.
But blessings on those who let you cry
unimpeded and beg to hear your tale repeated.
They are masters of mystery, healers, all.
Opening to pain,
enriched and enlivened,
they help us build true community.

How do they do it?
I've checked and so far
it seems those who can house pain
are always the same
who have taken their troubles
and opened wide the doors
fearlessly welcoming.

March 22, 2001
Seattle

Reflections on Glass

For most, windows are unencumbered
vision through.
For you, my son, they were pain of glass,
even without glare, an obstacle.
I go through days searching
to see what made simple looking so hard
hoping to find understanding, instead
see only layer upon layer of imaging.
Car plate glass concave swooping
takes the world and folds
pressing passing images from being into
nothingness.
Bus stop waiting wall clear
alternately reveals or hides
depending on what lies beyond.
Dark car passing the man seated near
is suddenly mirrored in front,
once past, he disappears.
Riding the bus perplexing layers of being
confound; windows show opposite street sides
moving at different rates
communicating distance
yet present simultaneously
along with still interior, peacefully coexisting.
Long ago train ride, door panel open
right angle to window
saw past and future merging at high velocity
in a line, Euclidean edge
of absolute stillness
empty of content.

So how does one make sense of all this
and who is to say what is real?
It seems eyes alone find no meaning
simply mirror reflections of reflections,
compounding confusion, fun-house illusion.
But enter the heart and the imaging morphs
meaning jumps out, startling.
All along it was waiting
for the organ of acknowledgment,
cipher of secrets, true vision.
Was glass a reminder
metaphor membrane separating body prison
invisible to most simply because
we do not see it?
No answers for me, no peace made of reason
but I am learning to see with my heart
and that is bringing me healing.

March 24, 2001
Seattle

KUAN YIN TEA HOUSE

I remember this space,
long ago boat trip in Japan
on my way to Kyushu with friends.
Awoke early,
couldn't sleep wedged between
where there really was no room for me
so I went up on deck and
logged passing minutes in diary
noting dawn's coming
increment by increment.
Misty gray sky met steel gray sea
at horizon indistinct, merged
in a oneness entirely new to me.
Here it is again, now night enfolded
slight twinkle of shore lights distant
line drawing on dark
suggestion of horizon.
Hear the train approaching,
huge diesels pulling, sound
throbbing, filling the night air
with memories of my friend's son
who just this time last year
put himself in front of one.
Our beautiful, tormented sons,
my eldest, your youngest,
sacrificial lambs, pain persecuted
finding no place of peace here
fled to another shore.
On my way to the beach tonight
I passed by the shop where he once worked,
The Tea House Kuan Yin,

and thought how he served in the house
of the goddess of compassion.
It's so hard to grasp this world we are in.
Hard to take in and digest.
But my friend, you and I know
what it means to discover
bit by bit, a dawning
growing inside our hearts
far beyond the horizon
place closer than close
we tend temple gardens
and serve the source of compassion,
as we honor and hold all the children.

March 24, 2001
Seattle

Moving Light

Raining at last!
Dark inky blackness
surrounding the beach
staring out the horizon yields lights,
distant buildings twinkling.
What's this?
They're moving
ever so slowly
and almost unnoticed
light panels seeming pegged to that far shore
cross paths like constellations unhinged.

World of wonders unending
I sit here searching the distance
hoping somewhere to find
my own moving light
and reason for existence.
Know what I seek is not out there.
My focus is pointed in a direction
that will not satisfy what is needed
yet here I sit
mesmerized by beauty
unsure how to begin.

March 24, 2001
Seattle

Void

Friends want me back,
the old me,
happy-go-lucky, carefree.
This new character is hard to be with
prone to silent staring and crying.
"It's harder on us, we don't know what to do!"
lamented one who hasn't called back
maybe thinking it easier to just leave me alone
than to climb in the space I'm in.
I guess she's right
for as hard as your death has been on me
I am clearly the only one here
absolutely sure of what she is doing
that being gathering every bit of data
pertaining to you
and my feelings of late
documenting,
sitting,
writing.
No time for visits or pleasantries with friends
not meaning to be rude
I am all in my head
and heart
completely consumed
driven to record as much as I can
before you fade from me.
I know this behavior is futile.
You are gone and my efforts
will not bring you back
but somehow I have to keep trying.

There is real danger I may lose part of you
slipping through memory's fingers
like beach sand
fading,
for beyond frantic focus
my being is all air
out of balance
blown so far away by events of late
I have to put one foot in front of another
just to move
and then,
I've no idea where I'm going.

March 25, 2001
Seattle

PARKING LOT CONJURING

Is this where you parked?
Could be, I imagine looking into the night
from my car see back stairs
leading up four stories windowless side of motel.
You took your gear this way, I'm sure
avoiding glass, shotgun and ammo
in black plastic bag up to top floor,
concrete walled corner room.
You meant no harm
needing only to end the hurt
no one understood or could cure.
I know this and love you even more
for your courage and dignity
throughout your whole life
struggling to survive
beyond what most can even imagine.
But you, who sold a gun to my son
in such terrible pain he shaved his head
so his hair would not touch it
much too thin for his large frame
looking pale and unslept,
you, gunman, agent of death
who helped him find peace
I cannot hate you.
But I wonder, is this the only way
you know to make a living?
Come, let me teach you to garden.

March 25, 2001
Seattle

MY WORK

This is my work now,
tying up all the loose ends
following every suggestion, searching.
And it continues.
Just last week readying your car for resale
at the insurance agent's I had to leave it going;
battery dead it ran on a jump
and I dared not turn it off.
Took quite a while to do our business
all the ID collecting and me so spacey
I'd forgotten my checkbook
and had to run to an ATM
at the grocery across the street.
"Such a good car it should be easy," she said
and I thought,
"Good and easy so seldom equate."
That done I set off in a hurry
to find a new battery.
Backing, I noticed a foggy rear window and
auto-pilot pushed the defogger.
View in rear mirror made me scrutinize further
then I saw a message from you!
"See Ya!!" and "Hello," written clearly
and it turns out, on the inside, in reverse
so only the driver rear viewing
on a cold, wet day
with the window fogged over could see.
Frantic, I turned off the defog, too late.
Your great car's systems working
had already erased your last words to me.
I spent the rest of the hour ride ridiculous

staring in rear mirror, windows shut,
heavy breathing
trying to re-fog that rear window.
Needed to see it, some trace of you here
though I fear this carrying on
may be making your passing harder
should just let go
so you can find your future freely.
But there is in me a need to detail
every paper scrap, every thought and feeling,
any bit of relatedness I have to you.
Beyond this there is no help.
So ignoring all else I'll continue
till I can find my way through.

March 25, 2001
Seattle

POTTER'S WHEEL

Try as I might to have my will done
I have figured it out:
one cannot get in the way of living.
And no matter what effort I made to control
I could not prevent your dying.
All this need to manage, as if
you had no mind of your own.
Overwhelming fear masquerading as concern
constricts the flow of our loving.
Pinched and paranoid
all we convey is judgment,
misplaced fruit of unfulfillment.
Attempting to teach from this place
runs aground
trying to force life lessons
into vessels untried and unfit
for the barnacled beauty of our own bruised being.
Parenting child becomes
ungraceful chiding argument
for the young cannot accept our broken dreams
as the treasure they are
instead see only deficit.
None can take wisdom before it is owned
through the fullness of living
completely spent in the trying.
Grasping, we miss it
and each other.
The first of many times I learned this
I was sitting at potter's wheel

working sea sponge dropped accidentally
and discovered the silly futility
of reaching for that sponge
while the wheel was spinning.
It eluded me repeatedly until
holding still
it returned to me on its own.
Is there ever a still point
where all is made clear
and do we ever stop to receive it?
Till then the only grace left us
is to accept and hold dear
that beyond conveying and understanding
hands open, palms outstretched
welcoming.

March 28, 2001
Seattle

EQUILIBRIUM

My friend, who has in her life
suffered greatly
said to me recently,
"You are the Queen of pain!"
I think what she meant is
even considering a lifetime of pain
the prospect of a child's traumatic death
dwarfs everything.
Now that I'm living inside that question
I see
tragedy comes to us all
eventually.
There is no escape.
So I try to lean into it gently
to take it in slow
and notice
many
leaning like me.

And isn't it true that the vessels we are
take in and are filled
by whatever comes
like gas in a bottle
seeks equilibrium?
Pain is no different.
How could it be,
when even a stubbed toe
is a crisis.

March 28, 2001
Seattle

April 2001

People who were the greatest help were those who simply sat with me and listened. I needed to share my experience over and over again as I searched, trying to fit an inconceivable event into a scenario that somehow made sense. My world, the apparent reality that I had once taken for granted, was completely destroyed.

While a few people were able to genuinely be with me, for which I will be eternally grateful, others seemed to be acutely uncomfortable, needing to distract me away from grieving. But for me avoidance and distraction no longer held any attraction. It was clear that the life I had been living barely scratched the surface of the reality that now surrounded and flowed through me. Everything was alive with dynamic energy beyond anything I'd ever known. While there was enormous activity internally along with acutely heightened senses, I was physically debilitated and could barely move. It was a bewildering, exhausting time.

Few of us can be with someone in deep pain without an urge to "fix" what makes us uncomfortable. It's a natural human tendency to want to ease someone's pain. However, I discovered that the urge to fix misses the mark when it is our own anxiety we are serving and not the genuine need of another. How can anyone be other than what they are, feel different than they do? Trying to coax people out of their sadness because it makes us uneasy does a disservice to those who are actively grieving. Better to simply sit with and listen.

The things people say and do in response to suicide while well-intentioned are often sadly misguided. Mostly they mean no harm but simply don't know what to do. Our society is averse to any mention of death and suicide in particular. The stigma surrounding suicide flows like an undercurrent throughout society, largely unconscious but in evidence everywhere as one can see even in the phrase "committed suicide."

In truth, hadn't I done the same when my friend's son had died in front of a train? Hadn't I kept my distance, feeling tremendous fear at what had happened and rationalizing my aversion by telling myself I didn't know how to help? Indeed, it was a short nine months later when Colby died that I had my initiation and felt first-hand the cruel effects of the cultural stigma surrounding suicide. Frustrated by the insensitivity I now witnessed—and had once participated in—it became clear to me that I needed to help people learn what it is to grieve traumatic loss.

Finding little help in the company of others, whenever I had time and could muster the strength I headed for the beach or a ferryboat ride. In nature I could be with my profound grief without upsetting people who genuinely cared for me and wanted to help. Immersed in the natural world there was no pressure to be other than who I was.

Most of my connections to the world had ceased to exist. I spent much of my free time writing, striving to find a way to communicate what was real for me. Besides giving me some respite, writing became a tether, keeping me from altogether drifting away.

JUST SAY NO

The world is trying to get back in
to fill me up
but I need to slow down
and stay empty.
Don't ever want to return to that place,
calendar full
frenzy of activity.

Just give me a quiet shoreline
or stormy.
And a bicycle.
Where everything I need
is a short ride away
friends,
grocery,
quiet room on a bay.
Tell me, where is this place?
I'm ready.

April 2, 2001
Seattle

SAND ETCHINGS
AT SHILSHOLE

Love this smell of seaweed and salt brine.
Look! Sand etchings of bird, canine,
human feet passing this way to the sea.
Calm flattens the water
stretching all the way to sunset,
liquid light path reaches back to me.
Stubby trawler rigged top heavy, leaning,
swollen wake bodes a good harvest
coming into rock-walled, safe harbor.
I remember a month or so ago
I came here feeling a change,
needing to witness your leaving.
Gone before, you kept me company for weeks
flower messages on stair,
in cassette case out of place,
earring in the box with your picture
and I'd not put it there.
So many clues that I knew were from you
though some might try to say different.
It doesn't matter.
I know what I know and came to the beach
to acknowledge your passage
from near to farther away.
As the sun set that day it went behind mountains
igniting clouds in orange radiance.
At the very last moment a blue brilliance flashed
on mountainside opposite shore.
It felt like you.

Now here come the children
black rubber boots straight to the edge
and into the water
to toss rocks and explore.
Mom holds back watching her brood
as the waves reach out and caress.
What a mystery this life is!
So many beaches we roamed together
shouting and playing, your brother and you
as I held back enjoying the view.
Used to think, "If I can just raise my two children
it will be enough for one lifetime," but not true.
It isn't enough to provide safe harbor
for just a few
and no amount of planning can secure a future
no matter what we do.
Children will always kick off their boots
and mothers will gather together.
And the sun always goes
with night on its coattails
as the moon reflects, awaiting its return.
Like the moon, each must seek
what only they can do,
our deepest reason for being
and finding, follow through.

April 8, 2001
Shilshole

In the Groove

I set out early
falling easily into freeway groove
letting it take me
flowing willingly into ruts that once seemed
to bounce me about threateningly.
No resistance now, no need to hold tight,
all anchors behind me tires ride easily.
My headlights scan morning
time between dark and dawn
when the world appears
a shadowland of paper cutout
evergreens and mountains
solid matte black on cerulean blue
awaiting animation.
Coming over hills I head steeply down
to valley extending
like a lace doily of angel hair
lying in places where rivers are breathing.
Dawn approaching, radiant red jewel
nestled between mountain breasts
so like dusk I might mistake beginning for end
if I didn't know which way I was heading.
Nature, resplendent, is painterly mimicking
sunlight; broad stand of natives, tall
white-trunked birch crowned with new growth
shimmering silver
towers over fuzzy, shades darker red alder—
perceptual tomfoolery.
Cold out, 38 degrees the sign flashes me
passing at sixty, then 7:09
but cocooned in car I feel only the hour

driving since six, up at 4:30,
I want none of this hard-edged,
numbered conspiracy overlaying a world
where subtle gradations are the rule.
Seek only gentle, rocking ferry and a view.
At last, ensconced in my tabled seat
window perch, the rest recedes.
Now it's just me, a few gulls and
sea islands sailing.
Fellow drifters witnessing mystery.

April 14, 2001
Interstate – 5 North

WORLD PEACE

There is no peace here
as some would have it.
No, just an immeasurable,
passionate embrace
that sometimes crushes.
Not benign but active principle in motion
one step we are laughing out loud
open mouthed
the next we are like a gull dropped clam
bowels strewn across rocky shore.
This is a place of fierce love
and even fiercer craving for it
until we find what we seek.
But in that we are one—
an obvious fact
if you have ever been torn by a baby's wail
or felt your insides melt
with the heat of longing
or reflected even for a moment
on the beauty of a sunset
or watched the moon changing phases
and wondered where you fit.
Inevitably, we come to a juncture
where what is, and was
is joined as one with our being
hearts swollen with the enormity
of containing so much.
No way to figure right from wrong
in a wholeness that simply is
illogical. Everything turning and changing
instar to chrysalis,

good or bad depending on where we stand.
I cannot even welcome you to this madness
you, already here with me, ever-present.
Let's sit together
for a moment resting from the race
and acknowledge in each other
ourselves.

April 14, 2001
San Juan Island

SOUL FOOD

Sometimes this beauty
so overwhelms me
I have to stop
and take a deep breath.
Layers woven together
blue sky,
or gray
are caught on wave surface
while lifting soaring birds
who then plunge into the sea.
Each part a fragment
wrapped round the other
interdependent,
and me
taking it in eye filter
straight to heart source
and mind.
Soul food,
good eating.

April 14, 2001
San Juan Ferry

FERRY BOAT RHYTHMS

Huge diesels
driving ferry
forcing sea
swift against
boat bottom
cavitation
pounds like a
drummer beating
primal rhythm,
"Rat-a-tat-tatting,"
as I lean
into front railing
breeze blowing
gale force
against me.
Like a puppy
ears flapping
head out car window
hurricane hair
eyes joyful, tearing
I keep time
with the drumming
head nodding
toe tapping
wonder, "Why
aren't we dancing?"
as my eager body
is tuned
by the wind.

April 14, 2001
San Juan Ferry

WHAT PRICE

What a price to pay
for finding my voice.
A life lived timidly
fearful of my own shadow
always anticipating disaster
guard up
hatches battened down.

Now, losing one of my anchors
and the reason I kept afloat
all these years
parenting my beautiful boys
what is left to protect?

The voice I held inside
is finding new power,
new life
in the midst of these ruins
and like the phoenix
fear is gone.
Would not have chosen it
this way
if I could.

April 15, 2001
Seattle

Passing Moments

There is no moment that goes by
when I don't think of you.
Other things seem to occupy
but beneath all the dailies
I am tugged this way and that
worrying some failure of mine
caused your end.
Deep inside I know better.
But that does not stop me
from baring my breast
and two-fisted opening chest,
boney protuberance gaping and jagged,
to lay out the contents of my heart
for examination, as if I could do
penance in self-mortification
and thereby gain freedom
from this pain of never knowing
did I do enough
or anything to really help you?
What is the end point of this torture?
It does not serve you
and seems to come in direct proportion
to a forgetful disconnect,
lack of ground.

April 18, 2001
Seattle

$E = MC^2$

Is this what it is to be haunted?
Every place I go
where I know you once went
I feel your presence, as if
I could talk to you as I sit,
see your profile passing swiftly through door,
almost hear footsteps on stair.
They say there is no place absent of spirit
we are just matter too dense to notice
subtle presence, a change in the air,
insistent knocking just over there.

But I feel gentle pressure
seeking acknowledgment
guiding my footsteps
each time I pause, unsure.
Energetic beings, we,
drowning in matter.
No wonder this life is a frenzy.
We speed ever faster, hoping
like insects
to cast skins outgrown
longing for release
from this glorious prison.

April 24, 2001
Seattle

Road Kill

It must be spring.
Saw several baby possums
on the road today
barely recognizable
gray fur smears
under tires.
Unfortunate reflex,
stone cold stillness
as if inanimate
passivity crafted
through eons creativity
serving survival's needs
now seems dull witted
and slow
in the face of our
unrelenting need
for speed.
Feel like creature
unsuited to my breed
whipping in and out
of traffic,
dodge ball frantic,
as if there were some way
we could escape
this massive,
metal flow.

April 29, 2001
Seattle

SOLITUDE

It was not until
you were no longer here
that I could actually see you.
Before, my hopes for you
and dreams
obscured my vision.
Now I reach
trying to find your familiar face
and laughter filled glance,
kind habits
but find only air.

Sometimes sitting here
quietly
my solitude is so deep
and rich
it almost seems you have come
and made a visit.

April 29, 2001
Seattle

Noticing - Day 121

I notice in others
a need to make my pain disappear.
Maybe for fear of feeling
or perhaps the notion that happiness
is free of it?
But I've found pain ebbs and flows
like the tide,
never linear, there and done
instead it's a circle wrapping
round and round
arriving back where you began.
When pain comes in some ways
there is a softening
as distance from the source increases.
But in others it's always the same,
much like in the beginning.
It comes lightly tripping
triggered by some small event
a picture, melody or passing comment.
And there you are,
ground beneath collapsing,
falling away as once it did.
In this fabric of life
cloth cut unique for each
we share these threads the same.

I notice in me an ebbing of interest
tide come and gone leaving me
high and dry
without a clue as to how
or where I should go from here.
No desire to engage as once I did

whether fashion trend or world crisis
it matters little.
Still, tethered to this shore
I continue to continue
feeling to a large extent
like a plodding, harnessed animal
grinding down my hooves on pavement.
That which does engage is other:
a will to learn beyond my current borders
to feel the moon's pull, energetic forces
and to listen to unseen voices.

April 30, 2001
Seattle

MAY 2001

Difficult things happen and we are left to sort out on our own what comes next. For those of us who have held the idea that we are in control, the dawning that we are not can come as a shock. As hard as it was to experience loss, being attached to the idea that it "shouldn't" be happening I actually made things worse, effectively digging myself deeper into a place of despair.

People ask, "How long does this suffering continue?" Looking back to the days of my greatest suffering I can only offer, "It takes as long as it takes." Though we may want the anguish to go away, one cannot rush healing.

My suffering came from wanting things to be different than they were, from being unable to accept what was true. There had to be something I could have done! Every "what if?" and "if only?" is a subtle form of imagining that somehow it is in our power to change the course of events. I exhausted myself searching for answers before I came to a place of recognition—there were no answers to my questions.

Though ultimately there may be no answers, I found wisdom in the search itself. Each nagging detail worked on me like waves pounding against the shore as I exhausted myself searching for some explanation, some resolution. Only after my last ounce of energy was spent did it dawn: things can happen that are beyond my control. When I finally arrived in the present moment, empty of all assumptions and imaginings, it became possible to hold what IS close to my heart. When one has loved deeply, finding the path to this place of surrender is a difficult journey. It hurts, but it does eventually get better.

Avoidance was impossible, I had to touch in with what was real for me. Even so, the touching in happened in small increments, tempered by long trips to the San Juan Islands and the beaches of Puget Sound where I found some respite from the exhausting work of grief. Opening to what IS, requires patience, perseverance, discipline and deep compassion when that opening involves enormous pain.

Mirage

Mercury mirage ever receding
slippery retreat in front of me
reflecting all manner of stripes
across as if the lanes went off a-kilter.
Silvery metallic seeming fingers
slipping around the bend
just as I approach again and again.
Is it possible for a reflection to bounce off
an illusion completely obscuring the truth?
I have seen it, that car, a full mile ahead
appears to be here, in front, where the road
dips down riding mirage stream bottom,
still water.
Then up the hill the car is suspended,
midair in the middle of dreamscape
cut-away hills hanging hourglass, empty
of the road between.
Liquid illusion banking and turning
dancing me down the road
giving previews of coming events
while thoroughly erasing the real.
Distant wheat field's past harvest stubble
appears and covers two lanes speeding
eastward, dry dirt path looming at seventy.
Road edge safety markers once buried
in snow now lift into space, hanging
in a shimmering vacancy.
At the very last minute the road
reappears solid again under tires
illusion of safety revisited.

77

May 10, 2001
Ritzville

Day 137

I'm losing it, my tenuous hold on things.
Strength once immense
is not what it used to be, one,
carrying a load meant for two or three.
I can feel my inner stability
which seemed like a mountain,
dissolving.

Had to take a day just to find some quiet.
Need this sound of wind in the trees,
sun rays dappled
playing through fir branches with the breeze
falling on my page like a symphony of shadows
dancing with the light.

The fire is crackling,
sound and heat bringing me seasoned comfort
to a place buried in memory of safety.
Feel the animal me returning to find
the patterns of time
hoping to regain my bearings.

Tasting tears the ocean is here
and I feel like a fish always swimming upstream
forever struggling against the current.
Surfacing now with a wound that won't heal
drawn into the flow, out of control,
lost, on my way to mourning.

May 16, 2001
Seattle

WITLESS

I don't understand.
In a world of cruelty and hardship
and just plain bad luck
what is this beauty that surrounds?

Where the amoral always seem in control
with sales to be made
and fortunes to be had
always on top of the witless
how does one keep an even keel?

Swept into the storm of living a life
searching for a shred of meaning for guidance
faced instead by dogma thumping
telemarketers hawking fashion trends
to the homeless
one's only recourse is to become so empty
there's no hold left to grab,
no place of attachment,
leaving only a mirror for reflection.

May 16, 2001
Seattle

Arrogance

Happy or sad
it doesn't seem to matter
I feel I am doing it wrong.
My failure at your leaving
has left me so deeply wounded
I founder in water and on dry land.
There had to be something I could have done
it had to be my failing.
Isn't that how it always feels
that our children are extensions of ourselves
and their every movement
our own?

What arrogance after all!
You were a person unto yourself
and your dignity will not be impugned
by my careless pondering and clinging
and reluctance to approach the real.
Even when you were five years old
and the doctor's news was frightening
my deepest fear was of losing myself
I was so tightly bound to you.

May 27, 2001
Seattle

Quotient

Is there some quotient,
something quantifiable
that must be rendered
following this division?
The tears just keep coming.
I'm sure there is a reservoir
that fills up every night
so the dawn is the beginning
all over again.

The grieving mother came to Buddha
dead child in her arms.
He told her, for a cure, to seek a mustard seed
from a house that had never borne death
but there was no house could fill her need.

All the walking and knocking
and talking she did
must have helped bring her body
to the place
her mind could take it in.

May 27, 2001
Seattle

HANG IN THERE BABY

Remember the poster,
wet, frazzled looking kitten
hanging by front claws?
Even it has a better hold than me
hanging there suspended.
Dozing in early evening light, drifting
in semiconscious sleep
I, too, am hanging,
desperate for solid ground
swinging somewhere between
beginning and end.

Four gently prodding daggers
address my naked arm.
Suddenly awake
I find sunny Leo beseeching
and say, "Leo, is it morning?"
No, just time to get up
feed the cats
and go to bed.

May 31, 2001
Seattle

June 2001

Researchers teach us that suicide survivors, those left in the wake of a loved one's suicide, are statistically at greater risk of suicide than the general population. Indeed, there were times when I felt that life had lost all meaning and my continued existence held no value. Given that feelings of guilt and worthlessness are common among trauma survivors it is of paramount importance to find a support system in the aftermath of loss.

Soon after Colby died I met with a Hospice social worker who told me, "Never let anyone tell you that you are doing it wrong." Her skill and encouragement helped me trust my own process when my path differed from what others thought best.

Six months later, I started attending a twice monthly drop-in suicide survivor group sponsored by King County Crisis Clinic where I had the chance to speak my truth and listen to others suffering loss do the same. I attended this group for several years and found it of great benefit. In the support group I discovered that for most loss survivors self-recrimination and feelings of guilt are the norm. Also evident was our basic human frailty, trying to off-load feelings of guilt at someone else's doorstep, for blame often seemed to be directed toward the survivor closest to the deceased. Knowing it is common doesn't make it any easier to bear the brunt of others' accusations or our own feelings of responsibility for our loss.

Eventually, most learn how to cope with the pain of loss without needing to pass it off like a hot potato but it takes time and help to work through these feelings and come to an understanding that holding onto feelings of guilt is another way of imagining that it is possible to exert control over another's behavior. As much as one might wish this to be the case, it is an illusion.

When seeking help, it is important to discern if someone is trained regarding suicide, for I found that not all therapists are equal in their understanding of or ability to approach the subject. The stigma surrounding suicide extends even to professional caregivers, a fact that many survivors are trying to remedy through legislative action mandating better training as well as raising cultural awareness for all. I believe the "doctor who carries the invisible lancet," that Colby warned about is simply someone who feels a failure if he or she cannot find a cure and thus needs to discredit our reality instead of admitting that something might exist outside of their expertise and experience.

Besides the survivors' group, mindfulness practice proved to be a life-line for me. Jon Kabat-Zinn, of Mindfulness Based Stress Reduction (MBSR) fame, gives an excellent definition on page four of his book, *Wherever You Go There You Are*: "Mindfulness means paying attention in a particular way: on purpose, in the present moment, and non-judgmentally."

84

Having practiced meditation for many years, it remained bedrock while most of my other activities went by the wayside. Sitting with the pain I felt, noticing my feelings without attaching any judgment or story to them, I was able to sift through and take note of what was true and what was not. Eventually, I realized that, in truth, throughout his illness both Colby and I did the best we could with what we knew at the time. This fact energizes me to learn as much as I possibly can about suicide prevention hoping that I will be able to inform and help others.

PARKING LOT — DAY 154

Parking lots seem to suit me.
I've come this far
and can't get out of the car.
So sleepy
I'll just doze here a while and watch
my liquid windshield
raindrop screen saver.
In front of me a forest stands
tall madronas seeking light
like coral lightening bolts
splitting dense evergreen.
In this place the dead and the living
are mingling with ease
every inch,
every micron,
a dwelling.
Scrambled chaos in perfect balance
how could I ever pretend to improve it?
Silly gardener playing god
planting and yanking with impunity.
This forest restores my sanity
remembering fuzzy edges that blend
one thing with another
and soil creatures, unseen
allowing our possibility.

June 2, 2001
San Juan Island

Survivor

You were gone and life felt done
but I had to keep making a living.
Had to keep moving along
lest those watching me
like a fish in a bowl
be alarmed.
My youngest son, barely out on his own
and finding his way so gracefully
is now full of ire,
estranged by despair at your passing
and blaming it on me.
My fault after all?
We will never know exactly
and there is no undoing
but with all of my failings
it's just me you see here
trying desperately to stay open
and clear
no matter the arrows that come winging in
lest I be left to mourn for both my sons,
one lost to death
and one to anger.

June 2, 2001
San Juan Island

Auto Pilot

Oft times I feel so dizzy
things seem to just slip out of gear
and I'm standing here
uncertain how to make the next move.
I knew what I was doing a moment ago.

Now the world is rushing, fast, past me
as I try to comprehend
which gear comes next
flying at fifty
down a road full of cars
and street signs and stores
and inputs galore.

Auto pilot broken,
no gauges but panic tracking,
as I try to grasp how I came to this place
and where in this blankness
I'm going.

June 2, 2001
San Juan Island

Unspoken Bonds

Smell of salt brine and creosote mixed,
magic tonic mending whatever ails me
here in these dollops
of ever green coated dark chocolate islands
I am transported to an uncharted world.
Always a shore bird
I recently heard
the massive wet
breathing of whales.
A joyous discovery coming half a century
into the life I've known.
And this seasoned crowd on first ferry,
sensible sturdy shoes and
Helly Hansons ready
possessing a casualness that feels at ease
in this wildness
and like home to me.
I'm glad I came back
to spend days among those
who love the sea
and wind in their faces
and relish the rainfall
needing that closeness.

June 2, 2001
San Juan Island

SONG OF YOUR PASSING

Drops pap-a-pat on broad leaves
gracing big leaf maple sapling
under the spreading shadow
of forbearer ancient
these trees give syncopation
to the music of the rain.
Across the path a fallen fir,
ahead a deer is sampling
nibbling new green
keeping forest floor swept.
Stepping into the meadow
silence descends.

Rain is still falling
on soft, yielding grasses
accompanied as always
by the song of your passing,
death's melody.
It's with me now
and now
and now
contrapuntal theme weaving through
buried in the song of my breath.

June 2, 2001
San Juan Island

WHALE WATCHING

As I sit by the sea waiting for whales
and just passing time I watch
people come to this beautiful place
and every one makes some pronouncement.
"See that over there, that tall doug fir…" and
"Jimmy! You don't belong on the other side
of that wall!"
From natural philosopher to frantic,
frightened mother
we share a common theme.
On the surface words differ
but underneath they're the same,
trying to fit what we see
into recognizable patterns
and if things don't fit we raise our voices
putting energy behind our convictions.
Listening closely I hear them, and me
being human in this place.
Despite all our expounding
we're like fly specks on window,
simply a link in the chain
trying hard to ignore
our deeply shared suspicion
that unable to control
we can only offer ourselves up
to loving.

June 2, 2001
San Juan Island

URGENCY

In front of the wave the world warps
and catches light, reflecting.
This urgency pressing forward
is driven it seems by the wake's energy
but I know different
because I feel it, too, coming through my body
warping the world into action around me
as if I were the ferry moving.
Deep sea upwelling from frigid ocean floor
looking glossy and calm on the surface
is really the heart of a storm,
a harvest of feeding and breeding
and on its edge is a ripping of currents
and moon tides moving,
waves cresting and surging.
Oh, to ride that urgency kayak on kelp bed
and feel the ocean breathing!
Rising and falling on sea chest
watching eagles breeze surf and whales breech
while glacial erratics sit island, stone silent.
It's the same with the ferry docking
and seeming at rest
just holding still in this motion filled world
takes the power of diesels turning
creating a glossy, upwelling calmness around it,
broad spreading surrounded by roughness.
That calm, precursor to energy breaking through,
sends deeply churned creativity to the surface.

June 2, 2001
San Juan Island

MESSAGE TO MYSELF

There are hints here if you will listen.
Quiet yourself, still those fidgeting hands,
sit for a moment
and take in your surroundings,
not those dreams broken or building.
Just this space as it is filled with layers of being.
With every atom of your body,
every soul awareness take it in.
Let eyes listen, ears feel,
hands open accepting.
Taste the acrid scented leaf litter decomposing,
the sweetness of soil building.
Hear the millions upon millions
of life forms living
and dying in each teaspoonful.
Look closely and see the crawling, slithering,
winged exuberance.
Wind and water players here,
sunlight and we, too,
and every step wrecks havoc
crushing a multitude.
But a balance is struck for so are we
innocent, uncomprehending our effect
and we in turn are crushed,
whether inanimate forces of concrete and steel
or entangled emotions, illness and pain
the effect is the same.
Be still and listen to your heart
open and take it in.

Let down the guard that seeks protection
nothing here is threatening
but imagination, dread filled
by an acorn dropping or a loon.
Release fear and open and then open again
till you see joy dancing, rainbow essence
animating all things broken or whole,
dead and living.

June 3, 2001
Seattle

GROUND ZERO

What is it that throws me off like this?
I never see it coming
and then,
all at once I'm dizzy
and drowning
in a deep salten sea.

Am I working too hard,
exerting to much to maintain
my balance?
Not eating right, too much or too little?
Or is this just how it is
climbing back
from ground zero.

June 5, 2001
Seattle

TEA ROSES

It's just a floor—neutral
but it seems to be mocking me.
All this gleaming and streaming of light
flowing through this long corridor
reminding me of years before
when I walked here.
Coffee and muffin in hand
I was in transit,
waiting on your recovery
from the fourth,
or was it the fifth surgery?
So full of fear I felt like screaming
but couldn't find my voice.
My habit of the time to smile over pain
putting on a happy face.

Is it cruelty for one so young and bright
and deeply knowing
to be so blighted?
Or are we like leaves on tea roses,
pulled off by the gardener
when she sees
orange,
or white,
or black spots growing spores
or little nibbles from larvae?

June 5, 2001
Seattle

Almost Normal

There is a "can't quite connect" quality
to my movements this afternoon.
Desperate for water,
forever crosstown through traffic
erratic, distracted turns and re-turns
I worry the person behind me will think
I've gone round the bend.
Whatever may be I'm in real trouble here
cacophony inside wrestling memories,
harsh voices shouting, "You really blew it!"
both for what I did and did not do.
A train passing so powerful
the ground is moving
or is that the wind?
Pigeons strutting and preening
a show in front
with a dark shadow background moving in
trailing long strands of moist, gray whispers
dragging along the bay.
Behind me seagulls are sleeping
one-eyed, on the ground out of their element.
I'll be okay sitting here. Almost normal.
The dizziness passes as long as I'm quiet
looking out, soaking in a darkening sea.
Thunderhead moving north
the ceiling is shifting and lifting
sky speaking gray volumes
ragged torn edges swollen with rain.

There's a little dingy running after the storm
sail reaching and taking so much wind
that at each tack back
the sailor is heaving her body up on the side
just to keep from capsizing.

June 5, 2001
Shilshole

Combatants

Just sit with it and breathe it in,
dueling voices,
blood letting inside my head
and heart,
salty river pouring down.
These combatants will spare me
no quarter.

June 5, 2001
Seattle

RUBBER BOOTS

Two days ago I gave your boots away
and as I watched those feet receding,
obviously delighted to have found
such sturdy,
size eleven,
steel toed,
black rubber boots,
I could see you.
The lilt of your lanky body
buoyant yet solid
whether twenty-two or ten.

Rubber boots!
For splashing in puddles
and working in the rain.
For mud pies and chainsawing timber
and exploring ocean beaches.
Truth is, I was always trying
to suit you in armor
and you really preferred Tevas.

June 6, 2001
Seattle

Internal Injuries

It's been almost six months and friends say,
"Come on over for a visit!"
I don't think they realize I can barely move.
What stops me I'm not exactly sure
but surmise there may be internal injuries
because something is pressing inside my belly
and holding my chest so tightly
I often get dizzy.
Suffocating with the weight of your leaving
my breath comes in Morse code
dots and dashes.
Dialogue running treadmill in my head
is pounding on my heart,
well spring of my being.
Sun and wind playing in the trees
are dancing boughs on the wall
and on my grandmother's cedar chest
home to a lifetime's treasure,
relics of my children's childhood,
puzzles and Legos and costumes
and toy trucks
safely stored for the next cycle.
Motion picture shadows swirling
sometimes distinct
then fuzzy hint of needles on twigs
seems even the sun can't focus.
Sound track wind rushing through trees
near, then drifting away
the swaying motion sunlight flickering
shines warm and healing on that cedar
while I sit here bleeding.

No one sees it.
They want to think it's done now
let's move on
ask me all the time, "How you doin'?"
and I say, "Hangin' in."
Two house finches are fluttering
at my open door, perched
for a second on rose wreath
and front porch light
next to the broken window I cannot fix.
My huntress cat, haunches quivering,
watches with interest,
separated only by the screen.

June 9, 2001
Seattle

Aware

I start each day aware of your absence
and end each day the same.
Something inconceivable,
your self-inflicted death by shooting
is weighing heavily on me.
Traversing the straits
listening to wind crashing waves into ferry,
looking at clouds wanting to rain
hanging suspended,
I try and try and cannot take it in
and have to return here again and again
to find space to breathe.
It took a mighty dose of suffering
for you to want to leave.
If I could know your pain
my questioning would ease
but I never knew, could not take it
even when you showed it me
and now I cannot help myself,
so broken and discarded.
This leaving was your choosing,
your time by definition,
and I will have to respect
and come to terms with your decision.
But gnawing at me is my knowing
the world has lost a beautiful being,
best by any accounting,
and having witnessed a child of mine
suffer, and leave first
there is nothing more I need from living.
Time now to loose my hold on things
and concentrate on giving.

June 10, 2001
San Juan Ferry

OLD MAN

Today a heavily bearded,
grizzled old man
was playing Dylan at the Market.
I walked onto his stage as I passed
and he caught me with a lyric
so I stayed.
Knelt down to find a dollar to give him,
unzipping backpack and digging.
He sang beautifully even if
a few words were missing.
Someone minding
someone else's children
happened by and the eldest,
maybe three,
started deep bending
and swaying from her middle
so spontaneously,
a stout little reed dancing
to the music of the wind,
she made me forget my sadness.
This is how it happens,
life drags us back, laughing,
for another round or two.
The singer's face told a tale of hard living
I could read
almost without looking.

June 12, 2001
Pike Place Market

ANGRY?

My supervisor shared with me that lately
I look different, my expression seeming angry.
I searched my feelings, trying to fit,
but couldn't find in me
what gave her this impression.
I don't feel angry.
Another friend wondered how I could avoid
railing against the sky and I asked,
"How would that help?"
And anyway, when railing at the universe
we shake our fists in anger and I'm not angry.
Walking through days and nights
I'm often out in public
trying to put on a sensible face
for those who might happen a glance
in passing, wishing only
not to seem tear swollen and stained,
nothing else.
Having sold your car today
and taking time to be with this feeling
of losing you by bits and pieces,
standing at the back of the ferry
looking out and thinking
I felt my expression twisting up and realized
it must look pinched and strained
and angry.
But you see, breaking apart and falling
from the inside out
there's no containing the flooding.
I'm not angry. I'm just trying for a moment
in this public place
to keep the tide at bay.

June 12, 2001
Port Orchard Ferry

No Rescues Here

Gray clouds bunching like scenery props
stacked in a row receding
are darkening with tears on the undersides
flattened,
against an invisible ceiling.
I see seagulls puddle
round the reeking of our standing garbage
then lift in a hoard
intoxicated from feeding and
reeling out over the bay.
I miss my Tevas.
Meant to go to work and work all day
but my leaving midway
has me here with socks and laced shoes
overheating.
Sold your car today and I thought
I could jump on a bus and suit up again,
ready to dig back in the garden
but find myself water seeking.
My stomach hurts but not from hunger.
I did pass hungry people on my way
lying propped against the waste bins
staring at me, disbelieving,
as if I had something they needed.
The red and white Coast Guard cutter
is throttling up and speeding away.
There'll be no rescues here today.

June 12, 2001
Port Orchard Ferry

Too Good

I want to think you were too good to stay
but that would be a falsehood.
You were like the rest of us, real,
and your brother, your father, your lover
and me, we all share your vicissitudes.
Human like the rest
with great goodness
and failings
woven together, one cloth
lit by a luminescence indestructible
yet fleeting
like rose petals, so beautiful
and so vulnerable.
Now that you've gone
my tendency is to fill in the blanks
imagination creating
what I can't remember
or never understood,
justifying your image
on the pages of my memory.
As this made-up picture grows stronger
and you fade
it's easy to forget
life's backing and filling,
binding us together while pushing away.

June 12, 2001
Bremerton Ferry

SEAGULL

Jelly fish floating, continuous motion
tan hood flexing and closing
pulsing toward sea surface
all at once it's flip-side up and open
wide like a lily on a pod.
Pond still and ruffle-edged
your inside leaves are deeply blood red
as tannish filaments extend,
reaching for and basking in the sun.
After a minute or two
sea flower suddenly flexing
it's down and gone.
Purple starfish are stuck
like flung pasta on pilings
starting where low tide ends
and a seagull is nesting
on the ferry slip wing wall.

Coming in almost eyeball to eyeball
I would still have missed you
but for your fearful crying.
Heading out the tide has come up
and now, several feet above,
I see you seeing me
tucked between wooden pilings
atop a nest of straw and twigs.
I move away quickly
hoping to avert a crisis of the curious.
They'd be all over this railing, reaching,
hoping for a chance at your eggs
like Peter T. Hooper's scrambled eggs super
but without my help here they come

lured by the romance of a fore deck sea view
and seeing you, stand there staring and filming,
unmoved by your piercing cries.
I want to shout, "Give her a break, will you!"
and think, "Silly bird, to put your nest
so near the ferry,"
but then I see your brilliance.
Sixteen sailings daily
minus low tides that hide you,
briefly visible during dockings
and reachable only by hungry eyes,
never eagles.

June 12, 2001
Bremerton Ferry Slip

POLISHED MARBLE

Bus terminal cavernous
with halva-like marble
is making me ravenous
after a long day on the ferry.
Lights streaming across polished ceiling,
red wire low strung, electric whirr,
tires' rubber running across steel tracks
sized, I've heard, so the tram
will never travel here.
There's a flute concerto playing
and flickering like a bird
fifty feet above travelers waiting,
stoic and solemn
city faces on.
Polished shadows passing
polished surfaces.

June 12, 2001
Westlake Tunnel

ASHLEY'S ZEN COFFEE

"Coffee?" she asked.

"Sure, let's make some
but I only have leaded," I answered.

"Great! I'll make it. How do you like it?
Have you a measuring spoon?"

"No, I just ballpark."

"Okay but be forewarned,
I tend to zen darkly," she said.

June 15, 2001
Seattle

BODY BLOW

I cannot be with ordinary people,
I've nothing to say
as they chatter endlessly
about their children.
For you without who longed for a child,
forgive me.
Once I was just like them
touting my own
whether expounding on their brilliance
or some nest embroiling crisis
I never once noticed
you, sitting silent, looking at your hands.
My children, always the center
of my thinking and doing,
a tumbling, raucous existence
full of laughter, and pain.
Even when giving them space
they were my focus, anticipating
their nearing independence, a time
I imagined I could call my life's efforts success.
What twisted fortune this, to see my oldest
launched into death.
Part of me has been torn away
a body blow to my center
that has me hanging off life's
speeding fenders by a thread.

June 15, 2001
Seattle

WITNESS

There were times in my life when I gave
a fleeting glance at suicide,
feeling neglected and longing for attention
full of youthful folly believing
another could give me what I needed,
when through some grace it dawned on me
life was not defined by others' definitions
of beauty or wisdom, freeing myself
I found love for life again.
Now with your passing it's cropped up again,
the uselessness of existence.

Your reasons for leaving
were considerably different,
the noose of pain having drawn so tightly
around your neck and head
squeezing you into a space no one could reach.
Over years of thoughtful introspection
and meditation
while searching for a medical solution
all the while slipping down an incline
growing steeper,
you found life in that state incompatible with
any reasonable link
to what it means to be human.

I don't know how you managed
in the midst of pain
hammering your body
to delve into life's most puzzling riddles,
like an apple pared down to its core,
and still you found life beautiful.
Helpless, I watched the slow erosion
of your vibrant and striding health

from joyous loving and rollerblading
to a wan and fetal curvature, inconceivable,
and still you probed the human condition
with a lucidity and grace
I hoped would forever be my teacher.

Your note said you felt yourself a burden,
as if your leaving could be a blessing,
a notion that confuses me
since from my point of view
the toting of burdens is what we do
in loving and sharing living.
But I understand your act
as the only thing left for you to do,
an act of courage
and from your point of view
a kindness to the lot of us.

I see all of this like sun rays at dawn
piercing my heart with despair
that no could help you,
least of all me,
and if I were to leave in response to this
mine would be an act of cowardice.
So I remember when approaching the edge
and longing for an end to pain
and emptiness yawning cavernous inside me,
I will honor your living and dying by staying
present to every part of this mystery
called life and death,
whether suffering and pain
or ineffable beauty,
a witness.

June 17, 2001
Seattle

III

Desperate

Desperate,
and desperately reaching this morning
I called in sick, but I'm not sick,
not in the usual sense,
just wounded and heavy with healing.
Can't sleep,
though I tried to put this feeling to bed.
Food? I abuse it and feel my body thicken,
bloated beluga belly
but the vacancy there is never filled.
Nerves are rattled, jumpy and irritated
at infrequent sounds of clattering metal passing.
Someone shouts, and I'm all
alarms on deck, alerted,
but it's just the rental, college kids.
My head hurts a bit,
thinking feels allergy thickened and distorted.
My gut is loose and squirmy
and keeps me running for the toilet.
Breath is short, so I unhook my bra,
unable to take it off.
Wonder why on earth I put it on this morning?
Made a fire, with tea and blueberry oatmeal
on the side, cat in her place on my legs extended,
tucked in with me in the blanket.
Paper and pen standing by
but the old standbys are not helping.
What must look cozy and healing
to a casual observer
feels to me flailing despair.

Even the birds were weird this morning.
Heard a strange cry out back at dawn.
Not sure but it could have been
a raccoon screaming.
Or maybe a crow, who've lately been
crowding the rooftops on spring parade.
Especially the mother, raiding nests for two
newly flighted and ravenous youth, sitting
shimmering black on black tar roof.
Now a murder of them is gathered in front
in the two tallest firs, eighty feet up.
Maybe thirty or so are split into groups,
perched in multiples on new, sagging branches.
Alternately calling and bobbing,
synchronized dancing, one tree
then the other, over and over,
a pattern seeming of significance.
I would guess this a wake,
seen it before, the keening and dancing,
a social gathering in memoriam.
Indeed, when I looked out a bit later
saw mother crow feeding one baby
and knew we'd come full circle.

June 18, 2001
Seattle

TECHNICOLOR SPRING

What is this beauty too big?
Today I had to come inside
the weather was so intense,
sun illuminating everything
as brush strokes of pigment lay down.
Thicker and thicker the painting grew
till the greens of trees were a vibrancy
so full I had to shy away
while rhodies of florid Jean-Marie red
had their leaves silver-tipped in dew
and sweet-scented lavender lilacs
wafted across my view.
A rainbow of roses preened in the breeze
among glowing, late-planted dafs
and sky, in a blue forget-me-not wrap
grew deeper and deeper till all I could see
was tucked in a star-studded envelope.
What is this beauty? And this feeling
as if my body was being seasoned
or fermenting and expanding
into something new?
Belly pressure grabs and breath comes
in staccato segments
as all my movements are watchfully careful
having grown suddenly, very old.

June 18, 2001
Seattle

GRIEVING

First emptiness
and energy too intense to move, rooting me.
Then pain,
the kind where you double over in the middle
unsure if you will ever stand again.
Then the reaching, methodical and steady,
the plodding animal hoping
for the logic in detail to naturally reveal itself
and paint a picture somehow rosy
to cover the uncertainty.
Then the stuffing that will surely quiet
the hollow aching in my belly
for certainty was not forthcoming
and reason has gone out the window.
Now the dizzy wheeling
unsure where to go or what to do
I simply spin in place
but this is no Sufi turning.
More like a top run wild or a centrifuge
where instead of grounding in a single thread
all my parts are separating.
Six months in and this is where I am,
each phase born of the other
and frequently repeating.
Right now I am lost in a frantic frenzy
bouncing off of everything.
People don't know how to help me
and the only peace I ever find
is sitting meditation
which I can't sustain, even knowing it a friend.
Cannot befriend myself.

Instead, I seem to cling to the dizzy,
disconnected state where
I make wrong turns and bad decisions
and cannot stomach others' presence
sometimes even for a minute.
The only ground I've found for all my efforts
whether running toward or swiftly away
has been a knowing I will never find
that which I seek,
redemption through understanding.
With your leaving all possibility of that
left with you and instead
you have given me a gift
so beyond my ability to take in
I founder and balk
and wonder at your trusting me
with such a huge responsibility:
to accept what is for its "is-ness" only
and to acknowledge your right to your decision
though it grieves me sorely.
Never able to say your taking your life
the right thing, nor either that it was wrong.
Living with this "is-ness" only,
holding my not knowing
without judging either way,
is the hardest work I have ever done
and without a doubt the most worthy.

June 20, 2001
Seattle

SQUIRRELLY

Every time I overextend the squirrelly,
jagged jitters move in
and I almost can't reside inside my skin.
Simply put, I cannot spend
but a few hours with friends.
With all the best intentions
I get pulled out of myself
and stretched so thin
the elastic, overexposed to UVs,
ultra-violence to my sensibilities,
has lost its stretchy resilience
and any ability to return
to a remembered normalcy.
Normal is gone, maybe forever
and if I don't give myself
ample doses of quiet
I'm in for serious trouble.
Used to be able to carry one side
of a conversation but now, alas,
this bird has been snared
in a net of tragic proportions
so large I cannot see its end
and the entanglement precludes
most every sharing
I have ever known with friends.

June 27, 2001
Seattle

MARINATING

My friends have left,
run away,
back to their lives of endless details.
I understand.
When I was on the other side I did the same
unable to consider the possibility
terrified by a loss of such magnitude
I simply shut it out
and with it, friends who were left
to sort out on their own
a fractured reality, inconceivable.
I don't blame them.

My family has left,
run away,
back to their lives of endless details.
I understand.
Gone to nurse the wounds that refuse to heal,
unable to share the inconceivable.
I don't blame them.

There is no sharing this experience.
It's a solitary thing
where one cannot be consoled
or comforted
and must simply undergo marination
in a broth so salty
and bitter
no one will taste it.

June 29, 2001
Seattle

VARIATIONS ON A THEME

I know what this is,
felt it before, a variation
on a theme of being human.
There were times long ago
when my world fell apart
and I tried to reach out to friends
but no matter how I tried I could reach
no one.
They were gone
and I felt abandoned.
A few repeats of this scenario
and I think I've learned the lesson.
They weren't running from me
it was I from them, running desperately,
casting out prickles and barbs
to keep people at bay
even as I was sure I sought them,
thinking they could cure my discomfort
all the time body leaning toward solitude.
When your skin doesn't fit
and life bursts normal's bubble
and the phone falls even solicitor silent,
when there's nowhere left to turn but in
it's a difficult gift and key to the riddle
that finds us over and over again
till we open and take it in.
My body knows this, not to run
but my mind is so runner ready to sprint
life has to up the ante and amp me up
till I'm vibrating, a speaker about to blow
ready to jump out of my skin.

No one can help me when I'm like this
and I know now no one's to blame.
It's just me being human
learning my edges
and finding my way back to beginning.
I need to sit and breathe simply
without expectation
drawing in the hurt I feel
and breathing out a healing.

June 30, 2001
Seattle

Cycles — Day 182

A gardener knows this, lives it every day—
there is no need for sorrow.
My deep sadness keeps me company
it serves no other purpose.
Life cycles endlessly
growing and dying and growing again
up from the compost of yesterday's beauty
flowers and veggies and weeds and trees
and people.
And bees and insects, keys to pollination,
propagation, cycles repeating and
repeating
none more vital, all essential
and on earth's schedule, timely.
Sadness is an overlay
a human remembering and clinging.
When I fill today with the past or future
I lose now's creativity.
Fitting, since I feel lost
sitting on this couch in pain.
If I stay here long enough
today may run me over
teenager impatient with my dawdling
but the self-sustaining cycles witnessed
must move beyond this sphere.
How could it be other after all?
Endless renewal with no waste, nothing lost
and no need to pine away.
And no separation
just an altering of form along the way.
Help me acknowledge the joy animating

the forest, the sea, the garden, my son,
magnificent blendings of life and death
and altogether, one.

June 30, 2001
Seattle

Blessing

It's a brand new day
or is it?
Seems a lot like yesterday,
the pain and feelings of abandonment
the only ones who've not yet left.
Time is crowding me into a corner
spacious only in its sameness
and the absurd,
mindless madness mirrored,
this carnival gone sour,
has me utterly confused
and searching for a thread to lead me.
There's not one creature
to meet or greet
just hollow echoes in my head.
Need a guide who knows the way
for I feel danger here
lurking in murky corners
projected out before me.
Feel the world closing fast
my edges tightly binding
there's nowhere left to go
but in
and I, like a child,
am still protesting
even knowing this
a blessing.

June 31, 2001
Seattle

July 2001

There was no going back to my used-to-be. Most of the activities that had once meant the world to me now lay at my feet as meaningless rubble. The only elements of my former life that remained intact were my surviving son, close family, a few friends, writing and sitting meditation. I no longer recognized myself and had to start over to find meaning in life and the will to carry on.

The wounding I experienced was beyond description. The uninitiated could not fathom my distress. "Don't go there, put it away, it's over now," are statements that illustrate how disconnected some have become from the process of life/death, as if one could remove oneself from the pain of loss. At first I felt anger when greeted with this kind of blindness. In time, I learned to hold with compassion all the various responses that came in the wake of Colby's death. I learned that people were deeply frightened by what had happened and fear made them do strange things, some altogether disappearing and some only able to offer harsh judgments. In the past I had done both without ever being conscious that my behavior was the result of fear.

Anything that reminds us of our ultimate vulnerability— the fact that we will eventually die—seems to trigger anxiety and fear. When confronted by death many people respond by trying to push away their uneasiness as well as anyone nearby who happens to be standing a bit closer in proximity to the reality of death. I, too, had tried to boiler-plate my life, to shield myself and my children from difficulty but I did not find the safety

I sought and the walls I build around my heart and mind precluded my having a full awareness of what was happening around me.

The devastation of grief was harsh and challenged me to open my heart as it broke the bubble of my imagined world but grief was precisely the function that helped me connect with what is real beyond all conceptualizations, even fear. Through grief I discovered that there is not a hair's breadth between love and loss. I discovered that life and death are not separate but are a wholeness, an unending process. Grief helped me lose fear and see how all of us are the same, doing our best, often in difficult circumstances. Grief helped me find compassion in my heart for Colby, myself, Arlen and everyone.

The ripping away of my imaginary constructs, what I had once thought of as "my life," was hard to experience but with it came an awakening for which I am grateful. Opening to all of life was something I might have missed in my efforts to stay safe. Now I understood that there is no such thing as "safety" and opening to what is real is a gift beyond compare. I might have continued to live in an either/or bubble-world and completely missed exploring the depth of the mystery that surrounds and permeates everything and everyone. That I had to lose my son to wake up is tragic and heartbreaking, but in that breaking I have, paradoxically, been made whole.

To begin to heal I had to surrender and trust, deeply experiencing my vulnerability, holding with great compassion the pain I felt, while simultaneously noticing the exquisite beauty of the human condition and all of life, bitter-sweet.

It was not easy for me to hold the enormity of the mystery that opened me and to let it simply flow through me. The awareness was there inside of me, and still I had to work to open to it, letting go of my habitual thinking that would often tighten in resistance. As I struggled to stay open, my path was circuitous and full of pitfalls. When I would get distracted and caught in destructive tape loops of self-recrimination or anxiety, mindfulness practice gave me the tools I needed to keep coming back to what was real. Similar to any form of mental or physical exercise one might engage trying to build strength and skill, mindfulness was helping me train my mind away from destructive habits, toward health and well-being.

CHANGE

There was a change in me this morning,
even last night I felt it coming,
a glimmer of joy
deeply seeded
permeating my being.
For so long I've not felt it
for so long I've been in pain
implosion of my being
retreating fetal
to my bed.
Falling and falling and falling
unable to rise up standing
dragging my feet in circles around me
twisting and turning
like a feather on a string.
Today came an inkling
of a subtle change,
remembered well-being seen vaguely.
Tender small flame let me hold you,
still and empty,
lest you go out again.

July 2, 2001
Seattle

GATHERING

I used to think it such a waste
to wait till someone dies
to gather friends and relatives
and re-cement family ties.
I've lived long enough now to comprehend
the how and why of these things.
Flung to the ends of the earth and rooted,
immigrants,
there are no easy gatherings
but the celebration of our blood links
and bonding
continues as we leave
and in these rituals for the dead
we honor our humanity
truly knowing it good to have loved
and bitter the loss of those leaving
warmed by shared memories
and newfound glimmerings
that life's purpose was never simply joy
but the tempering of our metal
through pain.

July 3, 2001
Whidbey Island

FISHERMAN'S TERMINAL

A memorial sits
next to my favorite breakfast haunt.
It's on a pier where rock songs blare
from a nearby speaker out to working boats
moored, and waiting for the season.
Seagulls are soaring, circling,
searching for food bits and fish guts
their cries
like homing pigeons
flying straight to my heart.
I have never been a sailor
but I come here and
fingers following
touch the fish forever circling,
caught in cast bronze,
and stand, a shadow
in front of names I never knew
and still they touch me.
Hopping sparrow, hoping for crumbs,
flies off in a hurry finding none.
Canadian geese, majestic,
long-necked cruisers on green effluent
reach out and gingerly nibble
insects and eel grass.
Across the ship canal
they'll be scrapping for french fries
but here they float, regal.

July 7, 2001
Fisherman's Terminal

Pain

Physical pain has never been
part of my vocabulary
but I just tweaked my right elbow's
funny bone
and I'm getting an education.
Not sure how it happened.
Pivoting into the bus seat
I guess my backpack buckle caught it
and suddenly my stomach knotted up
as if I might lose it.
It made me think of you
continual pain in your neck and head
you said on a scale of ten, seven,
topped off with migraines
taking you to nine now and then
as if you needed more stimulant.
How did you hang on as long as you did?
For two and one-half years you suffered.
Just now I felt I might have to die
and it only took me a minute.

July 7, 2001
Downtown Bus

The Walla Walla

Summertime and I'm riding top deck,
wind blown, watching gulls sky surf.
Effortless balance, heads swivel,
scanning this way and that, eyeing me.
Light gray wings, white head and body
I watch with respectful envy.

People's babies are toddling the decks
and my heart skips a beat
as they lean on the railings,
mothers standing back laughing
trusting the universe
never guessing how fast things can change.

Slight twitch, a change of pitch
and a gull swings wide and away.
Efficiency of movement so brilliant
it returns gliding and passing
without a single wing flap.
Moving mountain giving lift to the wind
has gulls out cruising this evening
joining me all the way to Seattle
spending barely an ounce of energy.
Feet tucked into feathers
snug up against tail
unlike the heron's legs bobbing and dangling
these birds are pure aerodynamics
as they sail, joy riding the ferry.

131

July 7, 2001
Winslow Ferry

VIRTUAL REALITY

Sometimes the most important thing I do
is getting out of bed.
I lie here imagining all activity possible,
a hundred different ways to go,
people to call and then
I stay like a lump on a log
virtually immovable.
I used to be up at dawn, engaged
energy levels so high I scared some people
and the cats, of course,
who would scatter in terror.
There is work to do that is not getting done
like going to the beach at sunset
and my garden, always a treasure to me
is languishing, buried in weeds.
My friend looked and said, "I've never seen
your garden like this." And I replied,
"I want to see what happens."
Like the story where the heroine falls
and finds herself in wonderland
you don't need a computer and screen
to wake in virtual reality.
The strangest part is this version of real
is more vital and essential
than any I have ever lived
and looking around it is clear to me
I am surrounded by the virtual.

July 8, 2001
Seattle

DREAM CHILD

Long ago dream child,
terrified,
running for help and falling
before father and mother
found she could utter
no sound.
Could not reach them where they stood
smiling,
genuinely puzzled
by her anguish.
You ask me how I'm doing
and I try to craft
a link between us,
lengthy worded explanations
but can find no portal entry
compatible with my circuitry.
Rendered speechless I flail
as if in dream
and terrified to feel so lost and alone
standing in the company
of family and friends.

July 13, 2001
Seattle

Not Soft

Not soft, this woman, not a chance.
Growing up wallpaper among social addicts
with the usual blissful and broken childhood
shared by a family who did the best they could,
a sleepy child till she bore her own,
awakened from hibernation a she-bear ferocious
when it came to protecting her young.
Echoes of this story reverberate across every borough,
a culture lost in its own excesses
acknowledging only the surface
as if we arrived whole with nothing to learn,
as if learning came without falling and pain.
Glossy lipstick smiles applied
to cover the discomfort no one speaks of.
Must not speak for fear something deep
might be unleashed and shred us as we stand,
wholly unprepared to face the simple truth
of your death, or my death,
as if we could control these events
by crowding feelings into locked down bodies
ever vigilant.
But whatever the sky needs to do today
is just alright with me.
I don't need to arrange it anymore
those days are gone forever.
And anyway, I find standing in the rain
a refreshing break from all the sunny deceit
that flickers on every box, human and inanimate.
Some think me hard.
Is that so?

July 16, 2001
Seattle

Mirror

The sea is a mirror
where all nearby colors
reflect
but more than this
the sea is present
in colors so changeable
and beautiful
it's hard to grasp.

We, too, are mirrors
reflecting on each other
and yet,
there is something inside
that bends light
so the mirror we are,
just like the sea,
always has the tint of us.

July 19, 2001
Seattle

No One Sees It

There is an itching around my heart
like a wound that's healing itches.
I don't know why no one sees it,
that wound around my heart.

There is a sinking in my belly
as when learning of someone's pain
you feel your insides dropping down and out.
I don't know why no one sees it,
my hollow, Dick Tracy belly.

There is a sadness in my eyes
that keeps me tearing,
like a dust storm, choking.
I don't know why no one sees it,
that storm swirling round my being.

There is a slowness to my step
a weariness weighing heavily on my feet.
I don't know why no one sees it,
the weight born of your leaving.

No one sees it.
They see my body and think me whole,
see me working and think me here.
How is this possible?

July 19, 2001
Seattle

Compost

The phoenix rose from ash
renewed
but I'm not ashes yet.
Just a heap of compost
working.
I feel the heat
but it's a slow bake
nothing so romantic
as alchemy.
Life is leaning on me
and molding my edges
till I fit that place
I chose from the start.
If only I could find it.

July 23, 2001
Seattle

Favorite Song

Like a scratched record skipping
and stuck in one spot,
I may wear this lifetime out
before I reach the end.
We're meant to go on,
there is more on the record
but what of these ruts that seem to snare
and hold me as if I was frozen in time?
Where do we find strength to jump the ruts
yet keep from overcompensating
and spinning off at speed?
A delicate balance must be struck
to follow the grooves scored on our being
without digging them deeper still,
or indeed, bouncing past
and altogether missing the music.
The record will eventually renew,
we are alive with that possibility.
Trouble is when the broken part
becomes a favorite song
or when we pretend we have no grooves
and blindly bounce along.
Broken we're no different from the rest.
Simply human.
Simply beautiful.
Simply best.

July 23, 2001
Seattle

BIFOCALS

Damn bifocals, cementing my vision
in a blur of confusion
as I try to get a fix
on this situation.
They've gone.
Flown,
in one way or another
and my sitting here
blindsided
is beginning to appear
to be something
I must deal with.
Chocolate tonic is not working.
I feel like a stuffed Thanksgiving turkey
and yet the pain
I meant to drown remains
and like that bird
I am eviscerated,
life altered beyond my wildest dreams.
Who on earth would expect
a trussed turkey
to rise and walk again?

July 23, 2001
Seattle

As If

Somewhere along a lifetime most are broken
but we pretend we are not
taking up armor and masks
as if so doing we could fool the rest
as if a state of brokenness
was something to be ashamed of.
Contorted behind a smiling
and daily polished patina
we bend ourselves into pretzels for fear
a glimmer, warm and needing,
might shine through and blow our cool.
As if no one could read the details
running ticker tape across our foreheads.
As if none could see our clumsy antics
tripping over bloated and rotting
unattended business.
As if our single-minded hypocrisy
caused no pain.
As if we could hide from who we are,
as if who we are was hiding.
And still we are loved by those who see us
better than we see ourselves
love letting go of face forever
and taking up the heart of us
however broken.
Perhaps it is time to accept
that broken is a part of place
that within these learning fields on earth
broken is a state of grace
wherein opportunity exists to learn the best
and the worst of it.

Perhaps it's time to recognize
and embrace the way we feel.
Picking our broken pieces
off the ground of being
learning to knit them together again
with compassion for ourselves
larger than we were before,
larger than we ever imagined
building with a new awareness
that somehow broken opens a door
invisible before.
And with newfound wholeness, expansive,
that embraces the broken and the mending
we become alive to the possibility
of sharing our humanity.
Unbroken we can never know this.
So let go of fear of falling,
stubbing pride and dignity
embrace the lessons a lifetime brings
laughing and crying wholeheartedly.
To ride our time without a bump
in our imagined being
would be to live an epoxy bubble,
brittle, indifferent, and unmoved by beauty
untouched by an ocean of love surrounding,
beckoning us to jump.

July 24, 2001
Seattle

The Garden

A big stack of dishes takes time to do
so I take the time to do it
and building a garden or raising a child
is a labor of love that never ends
so I give ample room in my life
to the living heart of me.
The familiar we accommodate
as we go about planning our lives
but how many are prepared
to make room for a grief
like the untimely loss of a love?
And how long does it take
and what space do we make
after sharing a lifetime to leave it?
Every part of your day affected
from the way you wake to going to bed
when you love someone
they are part of you
your every movement linked
so deep you don't think it.
It just is, like they are,
and surely will always be.
But people go in untimely and tragic ways
leaving us to grieve
a loss so large most cannot conceive it.
And yet, there it is and here we are
gathering days in bunches like bouquets
as we sit in stunned silence,
numb to ourselves and to each other,
numb to the dishes and the garden,
unable to move and barely to breathe

this grieving is work like digging ditches
and it takes all my strength just to sit.
I don't understand this, I'm still new
but it's pretty clear that one year or two
will not get me through.
And I have a feeling that this loss is living
like a garden that needs my attention
and the space I must make to live with death
will require a daily commitment.
Don't fear you may remind me causing more pain
there is no moment I forget.
In fact, the opposite is true.
If you can join me in my garden, grieving,
together we may find a healing.

July 24, 2001
Seattle

GOOD GRIEF

Got a dead pen
and some dead coffee
and pages used up,
a dead notebook.
Good grief.
Is that what this is?

July 24, 2001
Seattle

KEY OF SEA

A man is walking, twanging,
in the key of G
traversing up and down the beach
searching for his fortune
in soft sand by the sea.
His instrument sounds like
one string strumming
as he scans the dunes
for coins around him.
Following is his wife, I guess,
standing silent and ever present.
It may take two to find a fortune
or maybe theirs is them.
On my left, down one hundred feet or so,
two young men are playing a guitar
open fretted
and banging frantic rhythms,
no doubt searching for something.
It's what we do best, we human beings.
My instrument, in the key of sea,
is rising and falling, waves on the beach,
a melody of liquid motion
tuning the deepest part of me.
And my fortune?
I suspect it rests inside,
a mystery I'm exploring,
sitting
like a sand creature
silent.

July 24, 2001
Shilshole

Sea Story

Tide, reaching for the sunset,
has gone out below the white line, chalky bits
of crustaceans and green strip of shredded seaweed.
One particular bird, black banded head
and narrow gull wings, graceful,
is flying, scouting up and down the shallows
and diving now and then, working dinner.
Sky's clouding up, there'll be rain tomorrow surely,
gray icing thick with scallops of mist
across its entirety.
This living being, from curved sandy shoreline
to marina full of sticks, to green headlands
and lighthouse, sky's varied textures and colors
the complexion of which is so subtle
in shades of gray ranging all the way
from white to black,
this wholeness is so beautiful
my body sits dazed with wonder.
A tug is pulling cargo fast, six stories high
containers, blowing north with the wind.
There's a chill in the air as if it knows something
as absorbed lovers walk in twosomes
as small children wade and watch each other
as moms nearby build a fire
crafting some Friday night fun.
Wind steady, my hair is whipping,
tuned to the currents around me.
Ashes from bonfires are drifting by
going to join the sea.

July 27, 2001
Shilshole

SEAGULLS

The guano is gradually layering up
on the Bremerton ferry slip wing wall.
Two baby gulls hatched six weeks ago
are still sitting there very quietly.
Feathers of tan and gray camouflage,
feet black, while mom's are pink,
their down is almost completely gone
just a bit of fluff on their heads.
Mom was gone, too, when I first appeared,
a big difference from my last visit.
She arrived with one small squawk at me
that's all, no cries of alarm of flurried flying
her job is almost done.
A tiny dot of red near the end of her beak
disgorging something dry and yellow
this once vigilant gull looks pretty laid back
sitting on the wing wall.
Her youngsters blend well
with the gray of the wall
and the rotting debris of their lives.
Other travelers on deck missed them entirely
though the birds were in plain sight.
Almost as big as mom is now
soon they'll be teenager fledged
and join with the flock, all red spotted beaks,
riding the wind off my window.

July 28, 2001
Bremerton Ferry Slip

LEAKING

We live together, working and playing
but how often do we share?
We smile greetings
carrying on with the business of living
each with burdens, laden.
And now and then something leaks out
like a pressure cooker venting.
Let's take a lid off the notion
that imagines self-sealing
healing.

July 28, 2001
Pier 55

NIGHT WALK ON PIER 55

Dark is setting in early tonight,
sky overcast with low slung clouds
of loose mist like cotton batting.
The ferry just leaving is attracting a crowd
of seagulls flying out
from the darkening wings.
Aglow like a cake with candles afire
I see shadow people lining the decks
and leaning on railings
gazing back at the city skyline.
From the pier where I stand
the sea appears calm,
no white caps or waves are visible.
Just dark glossiness gleaming
under nearby lights
stretching out toward an inky horizon.
Wishing ever to be nearer the sea
I walk down the access ramp
and find swells so broad
they don't register as waves
rolling under a patchwork float quilt
rocking and rolling floats and boats
making my walking there difficult.

July 28, 2001
Pier 55

SOCIAL BEES

We can read each other's stories
written loudly across our foreheads
and like a honey bee's body wagging
the message is understood.
And like bees, we wander
lives of gathered experience
yearning to tell our tales
and be joined by shared significance.
Longing for and not knowing how to find it
drives us, hoping for a tie to bind us.
Like social bees who need the group
we hunger for the hive.
Even the solitary ones among us,
those mason bees who nest apart,
in the deepest sense no lives are singular
we're all in this connected.
The links play out like waves on water
crossing continents.
I know this, because the times
I've felt truly understood
it came as something visceral,
a knowing fed by deep communion
harbored in a look or energetic feeling,
seldom words or explanations
that union came from shared experience
that could be felt at a distance.

July 29, 2001
Seattle

AUGUST 2001

Grieving is a living process that cannot be rushed, a process that affects every fiber of one's body and aspect of mind. The physicality of grief surprised me, and taught me that I needed to make space for my body as well as my mind to work through the loss I felt. I soon learned that tightening against discomfort only prolongs those feelings. Instead, I needed to open to whatever was present, to let it move through me unobstructed by any ideas I might have about what it meant.

The sensations didn't have a story, they were simply there, inside me. There were causes and conditions that gave rise to the sensations, but invariably the root causes were not the reasons I was ascribing in my knee-jerk, habitual way. Allowing and becoming deeply curious about them, I approached the feelings asking myself, "What is this weight on my chest, this tightness in my throat?" Opening the door to sensations and feelings helped me approach and tenderly hold the deep longing that ached inside of me. My habit of attaching a story to the longing was so strong I had to work to simply rest in the feelings, without adding any explanation regarding them.

I did this work in small increments very gently and slowly, always coming back to my meditation mat, bringing my greatest difficulties to the cushion. By breathing and relaxing into the sensations inside, I could begin to discern what was true and what was imagined. Focussing on the sensations and letting go the stories I associated with them helped me see how my imagination was circling in remembered patterns as well as in anticipatory fear, neither of which had any relation to what was happening now.

Simply relaxing in a safe place helped me begin to understand that my body had real information for me that I was missing when braced in self-defense. Opening to the sensations was like learning a new language. Gleaning the full import of the messages my body was sending took time but by relaxing on the path of discovery, my awareness of what was true deepened. Giving myself time to do this work was vital.

After the initial numbness of shock wore off and the strange energies that were swirling through me subsided, I felt as if there was a dark, cavernous emptiness inside of me. Trying to sit with what was true, to rest in that emptiness, was uncomfortable and frightening at first. My son's death was slowly teaching me how to make peace with the paradoxical nature of life. From my experience on the night Colby died I knew in my deepest being that "There is nothing wrong," but that knowing stood in stark opposition to the fact that "Everything is wrong!" How to hold those two perspectives in equilibrium was something I could not reconcile in the beginning.

Slowly, I began to see that my feeling "everything is wrong" came from my wanting to hold onto my son as he had always been, alive and vibrant and happy. My holding to that notion created enormous stress in my mind and body for the truth was, he is gone and no amount of my wishing otherwise could alter that fact. In time, I began to see that Colby's death was another facet of life as it IS. Not something I wanted, but something

151

that was true and was part of the wholeness of the world and all of us in it.

The one constant in life is change and learning how to accept Colby's death was a challenge that went to my core. While it does get better with time, being present with loss is a practice I have had to engage on a daily basis, learning how to hold paradox close to my heart. I was beginning to see what Colby understood when he said, "Life is so beautiful in its triumphs and tragedies. Everywhere I look I see it now. There is beauty even in fear and pain but visible only to those deeply submerged in it."

Life holds all things, the beautiful and the horrific, present simultaneously. Trying to shut out what I wished to avoid effectively dampened my ability to experience joy and beauty. Until learning how to work more skillfully with life's challenges, whether welcome or unwelcome, it was easy to get lost in my imagination, running tape loops of past regrets or what I feared might develop in the future.

Dwelling everywhere but in the present, I cut off the flow of life and became encased in a tight bubble of only what I would allow, outside of which was life itself, forever knocking on my door. When the bubble burst, as it inevitably does, there came the opportunity to explore what life really IS—beyond regrets and fears, beyond judgments and expectations. In the presence of this difficult gift is where I found myself.

As I Lay Me Down

So grateful to lay me down to sleep
and so sleepy,
soon the sleeping will begin
and dreaming, if I'm lucky
I may dream of you
somewhere
I can hold you for a moment
firmly.
One minute I'm excited
to be pushing beyond the limit,
the next hanging back
letting nature take me
where it would
but lying back
words spill into my head
and I have to rise up and start again
jotting them down, solid and flowing
as if they had some substance
of their own.
And then sleeping
the tossing and turning sets in
and waking, I wonder where I've been
for the clarity of my used-to-be
grows dimmer
and instead
my bed seems to begrudge me
the comfort of a friend.

August 1, 2001
Seattle

PARK BENCH — DAY 213

Sky looks quilted this afternoon
like a down comforter draped casually
resting on sky scrapers in the east
and in the west on mountain peaks.
Sea is dark gray slate and steel
that fast boats score and cut right through
spewing flake white froth in plumes behind them.
Wind across quilt is moving like water
leaving tidal flat ripples suspended.
Hopping a water bus to Alki
I came looking for a bench to sit
and honor you, remembering,
hoping to unload my burden
where the sea can help me tend it.
I had to walk a mile or two
there was nary a trace of the land bus
and it's funny how exhausted I got
as if I'd forgotten the load I carry
and forgotten how to walk.
Now gulls are out working the beach in force
and one juvi looks at me expectantly
checking to see if I'll play the game of food,
sauntering teenager, all attitude.
Waves rolling in are gathering steam
from the storm building in the distance.
Flying saucer clouds are sailing the Sound,
a show for those waiting on the ground
lining the banks and shorelines.
Children playing and riding big scooters,
hurtling bodies and wheels together,

are screaming like gulls as they scatter.
Now comes a hole in the clouds
with sun shining through
and I'm suddenly bathed in golden light
looking out toward a sea gone dark, indeed,
and I feel just like a kid
reading under the covers by flashlight.
Fisherwomen and men out on the pier
are spinning webs of nylon
as I sit bobbing on wooden floats,
like a cork or a piece of driftwood.

August 1, 2001
Alki

Tsunami

It's not that I'm always sad.
I can laugh at jokes sometimes
and even be playfully silly.
It seems I am mending a bit
don't feel broken through like I used to.
But sometimes when I think of you I
remember with a starkness
that cuts to my bone
how you died and that you really are gone
and I'm filled with an emptiness that spins
me around, a vortex of loss and pain.
So I just do one day at a time
writing it down as it comes along
not really wanting more than this
going to the beach whenever I can
to connect with the beauty around me
riding out waves and breakers of sorrow
rolling in like erratic tsunami.
And I need to take care
not to do too much,
indeed, not to do what I used to
because I've found when I start to feel
somewhat solid
I reach too far and am soon exhausted.
So I stay quiet and alone much of the time
an existence that's fairly tentative
but in regard to a world that goes
steamrolling by
this works just fine for me.

August 1, 2001
Seattle

THE CROW

Crossing the street the crow,
one careful foot in front of the other,
looked like a toy with wind-up feet.
Street of heavy traffic
oddly vacant
I guess she felt it deserved
a closer look.
Pecking once, then midway, twice,
casting a quick glance left and right,
it moseyed seeming quite content
surveying the territory.

Watching from bus while waiting at light
mind lost in thoughts of losing you
I sat cemented, wingless, in my seat
exhausted from my day at work.
Seeing the crow I wondered
how odd it is that a bird will walk
and a human being choose solitude.

But how else can bird and I discover
the hidden gems waiting, under cover,
out in the wide open, often trod over
yet inaccessible to our normal?
How else to seek that hidden
under our very noses
to find that flight, birthright,
born human of this earth.

August 2, 2001
Bus 65

THE BELL

This morning I heard the school bell ringing,
long and loud as I lay snug and sleepy
in my Sunday morning bed.
I could feel myself and the entire neighborhood
spring from our sheets and run shouting,
released, out to the schoolyard playground.
This simple sound of a school bell ringing
flooded my mind with memories.
And so it goes throughout our lives
nothing is the thing itself,
everything we see or hear
carries the weight of all we have lived.
My friend had a dream
that she was walking along
in a cute little leotard and feeling pretty good
about how she appeared, imagining herself
sexy and appealing in that tight little suit.
Then she noticed the weight of something odd
so she turned and was appalled
to find leotard dragging on the ground
distended several feet behind her
with diapers and dishes and all the flotsam
and jetsam of a young mother's rounds.
If I can learn to hear a bell when a bell is ringing
I believe I will be free.
One day I will leave solid behind
as I leave this earth and my human body
but if I continue to cling to a lifetime's imagery
I wonder, will it follow me?

August 5, 2001
Seattle

Empty

There are two sides of empty:
when I'm grounded and centered
empty feels good
but when not
I want to fill it fast
with whatever is handy,
food or people.

Knowing this I'm hard put to understand
how I get lost in the hole
of empty needing full but I do.
The resistance I feel to the empty that heals
is so peculiar.
Simply layers of habit
that lock me in patterns
so self-destructive
I can't understand the appeal.

August 6, 2001
Seattle

SIBLINGS — FOR ARLEN

We had little to offer each other,
consumed with searching our feelings
and reality for details to convince ourselves
we did the best we could
or, indeed, to bear alone our burden of guilt
that perhaps we could have done better.
It takes time, some longer than others,
to be able to share these things.
And it takes compassionate help
to unburden oneself
of a weight that has no substance.
Grieving sudden and traumatic loss, shock
and the tumult of pain are so catastrophic
you're twisted outside in and insides out
even living together you rarely meet
and so burdened with grief
you have nothing to share
and so broken you need intensive care
though few know how to give it.

I watched my youngest as if from a distance,
a strapping and handsome youth,
struggle with sorrow and feelings of guilt
pretty much by himself.
Just like me there was no way to reach him
my attempts were put off as invasive.
I understood this, since I felt the same
of people who tried to reach me
but so hard, to not be able to reach
for part of his grief has been anger at me.

So we've been grieving our loss
in a version of tandem,
parallel paths at some distance,
and when I'd try to reach out he'd say again,
"Mom, I just need space."
It must be confusing right at the age
when you're off to find your wings
to suffer the loss of a brother to suicide
and it must be confusing to be part of a culture
that has so little compassion for people
that suicide is seen as a blot on one's character
and good reason to keep one's distance.
But my youngest is an amazing young man
with a wisdom beyond his years
and gifted at disarming hypocrisy
by calling it like it is.

In the end we all live our lives alone,
working things out as they come along
but if I could give him anything
it would be the certain knowing
that his relationship with his brother
was like that of all teenage siblings,
competitive and often hurtful.
And I'd give him the knowing
that under this gloss of everyday normal
his brother loved him dearly.
I know this because I watched them grow
side by side through all their years
and I saw the fabric that knit them together,
whether one year stitched closer
or farther apart,
their foundation grew from the heart.

But I don't need to give him this,
as he looks over time he will find it himself
so I will give him the space he wants
to find his way in the world
and the certain knowing that
his mother loves him
like the ocean of air loves the earth
and I'll be right here and reaching for him
whenever he's ready to share.

August 6, 2001
Seattle

Moon In My Window

I awoke in the middle of the night
in the middle of a dream of writing a poem.
It woke me up, this trying to figure
how to write the poem of helping my son.
I will learn to get along,
I've had much time to build compassion
for the outrageous fortune a lifetime brings
no matter the struggle or people.
What I cannot figure is how to help my son
his entire life lived in tandem
every joy and struggle shared by a brother
adored from the beginning.
How can I help him piece this together?
What comes next and how does he carry
the weight of losing part of himself
and shared events, happy or sad,
what difference?
It all goes when the one you shared with
is taken from you by death.
How can I help him when people are cruel
and wrap ridiculous judgments
around an event that frightens
and makes them feel vulnerable?
How do I help him blend with a culture
so broken it moves to attack the wounded
when loving tending is needed?
And how to explain my preoccupation and
distance when he is needing my attention?
How do I help him see
how dearly you loved him from the beginning?

163

Even with childhood tangles
and teenage insults, behind these,
the deep love I saw, how do I show him?
And his anger at me in the midst of our loss,
how can I help him see I did the best I could?
I have so much water under my bridge
I will ride out the currents around me
but how do I help him keep afloat
and how help pump a boat swamped by loss
with nary a bucket to speak of?

This went on for a while it seemed
till finally I fell back asleep.
Arose late and stuffed breakfast in haste
trying to make the 5:30 bus.
Riding and pondering still, I sat,
head back as if asleep
then opening my eyes
I saw the moon framed
by the top vent window
looking much like the light
on the night you died,
clear and round and yellow
and suddenly it was as if
answers appeared in my mind:

Open your eyes, see the moon high above you
Open your heart to the pain of loving
Open your arms to hold him dearly
Open your mind to accept his view
Open your belly and breathe in his anger
Open your being and love him deeply and he
will get the message.

I jotted this down as it came to me
and went about my work.
Returning home at the end of the day
tired body and mind in afternoon tub
I lay back to soak my workday off
and looking up in the bathroom mirror
there it was again.
Hot bath water had steamed it up
but only the top half
with a straight line division
through the mirror's center
as if looking out at the horizon.
And in the middle of the fog
a circle was empty
looking much like the moon
in a mist might look
but this time the moon was a clarity.
I still puzzle how this could have been true
and whatever it means is immaterial
but I do know that the image was real
and helped me get clear about what to do
and we are, indeed, mending.

August 8, 2001
Seattle

RIDDLE

Please find it in your heart
to listen if you will.
I don't need explanations
of how to go about it
or where I should be by now.
I need to tell my story simply
and despite the painful sadness.
Sit with me.
I cannot give you how
or where I am
cannot fit myself
into models experts crafted
hoping to help me heal.
It doesn't help to have you say
I should be doing it differently.
My one and only clear goal now
is to sit here quietly
needing only to be
who I am
and where I am
the rest remains a riddle.

August 14, 2001
Seattle

Colby's Poem

In a dream last night
I kept revisiting
a poem unfinished
adding a phrase here and there
and a word or two.
It was as I wandered
through a life
fuzzy
and indistinct,
I kept coming back
trying to complete
a poem
about you.

I just couldn't do it.
Even with huge gaps of content
there is still enough of you
here
I can't get it down on a page,
your leaving.

August 14, 2001
Seattle

SEAGULL SIB

I came fully expecting to find them flying,
hoping I could see them
all the pleasure I'd gleaned
from watching them grow
I felt like a neighbor, vested.
What I found was so stark in its simplicity,
a beauty of a sort I'm getting used to,
it took a while to adjust my lens
to take in what had happened.
Next to the discarded nest
along with guano and feathers
was a carcass with gray mottled wings
splayed out and lying just so
I could barely make out scant fluff of down
stuck on a dried up head.
It lay there like a totem on the place it had lived
or a token in ceremonial burial.
I searched for the sib, scanning
shoreline and shipyard, feeling full
like when life gives you more than expected
checking every bird I could spy in the area
but nowhere could I find a brown gull juvenile.
The ferry moved out of the slip, returning
and in response to someone's offering of chips
the whole neighborhood came flying.
Among this flock was a single gull, brown,
no more down and flying with the rest.
My sigh of relief was barely audible
but carried a mountain of feelings

and I thought of the note you left
where you wrote, "Life is so beautiful,
in its triumphs and tragedies.
Everywhere I look I see it now."
Heading back home across the water
sitting on deck in the evening breeze
I wondered again as I often do
how did we ever lose you?

August 14, 2001
Bremerton Ferry

VIDEO GAME

A contrast on an order exponential this,
sitting at my computer, dusk falling softly
outside our windows, listening to my caring son
playing games of mayhem and bloodshed.
And as he plays he's chosen to listen
to music that tells a tale
about finding peace in the arms of an angel,
the gunfire coming from all directions
ripping and booming and screaming
so loud I should put in earplugs
with shouts of, "Fire in the hold!" ringing out
as the singer's sweet and gentle voice
the angel's arms enfold.
This is the closest we have been in weeks
my youngest son and I.
The gunfire is hard on me,
I have trouble unloading a lifetime's imagery
not the least of which is his brother's suicide.
From where I sit images on window reflect,
blood splattering across walls and steps
and I don't understand this amusement.
But the outlet is a comfort to him
a teamwork, internet involvement
and community building of a sort
that I am learning to live with because
I need my son
and he is teaching me to lighten up
and not get so invested.

August 18, 2001
Seattle

ROBBED

I have been robbed.
A violation of my being:
my child dead and gone
and this life I'm leading
feels like a dream,
a nightmare-vision world without him
where I continue.
You made me laugh,
Cheshire grin and playful eyes,
what a treasure all the years we shared
the three of us together.
I cling to my memory of you
like a raft on a great salt sea
the only thing left solid save for your brother
and my clinging to him in this time of need
may drown him in my suffering.
So I go to the beach and cling to the sea,
at least I cannot drown the sea.

All my cozy things surrounding
are now just empty shells.
I want to strip it bare, the walls and floors
and open all the windows and doors
to be able to breathe again.
The weight of life's accumulation
suffocating, stifling.
That which I cannot carry
I need to leave behind me.
This may be overreacting to a difficult situation
but there is about it the feeling of opportunity
I must not squander in safe assumptions
and habit patterns.

For once this hurricane is past
I might sink back into habituations
of overwork and recreation,
comforting to a certain extent
but ultimately self-negating.
Now I need to let things go
along with the fear I feel is building,
no need to let it in again.
I'm past pretending my efforts
can exert control
over a life's unfolding.

August 20, 2001
Seattle

BONES

Bones are bleaching in the sun
and the feathers have gone gray.
A rainbow dot hangs on western horizon
coloring a gauzy cloud ripped up the middle,
edges frayed and dangling, curling in the wind.
Dusk is falling fast and gulls are winging
back and forth, brown gull with the rest.
White gauze on blue is changing shades
as the setting sun slips behind mountains
horizon bursting into flame.
Now the clouds are of spun gold
filaments spewn across the sky,
as if a volcano erupting, violently
and the mountains are draped in a saffron robe
as the moon coming up close to full in the east
is following along with the ferry.
I stayed on deck till the sun went down
and the rainbow disappeared.
Wake on water is rolling out
across broader swells that are rocking the ferry
a gently swaying motion that
when added to the engine vibration
feels like a heartbeat inside a womb,
steady and healing and warming.
As I sailed away the sun was gone
and too, all color from the sky.
That left, was a rack of bones laid out
and a silky white kata
draped round the mountains.

August 29, 2001
Bremerton Ferry

COINCIDENCE

Out on deck, watching the sunset
the wind got colder and colder
so I came inside, wandering, looking for a seat
and happened to notice the picture
and recognized the place I sat
so long ago last year.
As it happened at that very moment
the ferry was passing the very same spot
where I sat writing last December
trying to convey to friends in holiday spirit
the difficulty I was having, without letting on
how truly desperate I was feeling.

Later that night you took your leave
and on the next morning, your life,
and somehow here I am again
this place marking a cycle gone round
a marker of made up significance.
And yet it helps me, the layering of water
and shoreline with mountains,
clouds shimmering, orange and filmy,
this noticing of where I am
the place being almost exactly the same
yet different.
I guess I'll always see this way,
the before you left and the after.
The place is still full with beauty,
at least that much has not changed.
At the time I barely saw where I was
I was so worried about you.
Now I can see a great deal more,
your gift to me expanding.
Sorrow is here and tears are rising
as the clouds lose color, going gray.

The view is becoming a shadowland
and I think of how we lost you
and the pleasure I found watching you grow
and my hopes you would someday
have a family.
Thoughts drift by and cause me pain
but I cannot question your leaving.
You did what you felt you had to do
and my task now is to build life anew
and when sadness comes to feel it fully
and then to let it go.
I have no illusion it will ever leave
nor would I want it so.

The mountains are crisp
and clear in the distance,
it's like this every day.
As the sun goes down the mist clears away
leaving a startling clarity.

Reflection people pass me by
as I stare out the window
a child with father following after
and I follow their image as they explore,
back-and-forth-father hovering close
trying to prevent disaster.
The picture reflects
seeming outside the window
as if it was hung in the sky
growing clearer and clearer
as the sky grows dimmer
and I sit filled with wonder
at this shadow filled world
longing to find what is real.

August 29, 2001
Bremerton Ferry

DREAM WINDOW

There is a window
where we can see

what eventually we must do.
Not around corners or through the years

look right in front of you.
What some have done

to navigate the stars
cannot be shared with you - present

together and all of one,
our ways will be very different.

When streams diverge
there's no need to fear

life must be discovered not given
and in the end no matter

the effort we might expend
none need protect us from living.

August 30, 2001
Seattle

SEPTEMBER 2001

When difficulty is severe enough there is no avoiding it. Back and forth I struggled until learning to stay with the sensations and new awareness accompanying loss, breathing into them, noticing everything, relaxing when my body tightened around an idea or my breath caught in my throat. In this laborsome way I discovered that leaning into, rather than away from what IS, is key to finding release from pain—a paradox. With this dawning I have been finding my way through the labyrinth.

The experience of traumatic loss helped me to better comprehend the Buddhist teachings I had been reading and practicing for years. Now I understood that staying present with what is happening is not meant to prolong discomfort but is a method of noticing what is true right now, and then following sensations to their source, creating enough space to observe rather than react to what is happening. Freed from judgements about what "should" be happening I concentrated on what IS happening.

Research has shown that our bodies react the same whether threats are real or imagined. As a result, dwelling on imagined fears can create enormous physical strain, effectively creating a state of perpetual fright-flight. Moreover, trying to brace against a perceived threat or tightening in response to a stressful memory, I would end up getting stuck in the difficulty I wished to avoid, my mind circling obsessively in tape loops on the topic of concern. Creating some spaciousness around my feelings gave me room to notice what was happening without jumping headlong into a reaction. Gradually, I could bring wisdom and compassion rather than reactivity and fear to what I was experiencing.

Due to our culture's inability to approach death or change as a fundamental part of life, it is a rare individual who can be truly present with pain. After trauma it is important to be with those who can listen without any need to "fix." I saw now that the desire to fix is another vestige of fear, imagining there was something "wrong" with the way I felt.

Gradually and gently allowing sensations to move through me was a kind of alchemy where my body and mind became the vessel in which love and loss did their work. Trying to avoid this transformation seems logical from the point of view that most hope to avoid pain. But by relaxing and breathing into the discomfort accompanying loss, I learned how to more skillfully engage the process of transformation that is life itself.

Similar to the breathing exercises that help when giving birth to a child, birthing myself through difficulty was not easy but was made more comfortable by relaxing and opening to the feelings rather than constricting against them. Focussing on the natural flow of my breath helped me relax in the present moment, as I brought my attention to what was real.

WHAT LEAVES?

Ah, Colb, I miss you being here, in your body,
and I miss Arlen, too, so far away at school.
Summer is passing fleeting fast
and I'm back here sitting on my brick red couch,
remembering and searching for clues to my sanity
as I try to fit back into society.
The couch that belonged to my mother, now gone,
I use, a passing resident
grateful for the way it fits my body
snug and warm like her cat, Artie,
fit our family before she took leave of us, too.
All these comings and goings
make me wonder sometimes
what exactly is it that leaves?

The obvious answer being your smiling face
and the way your wore your eyes half-mast
grinning like a Cheshire cat about to tell
an amusing story that always made me laugh.
But a while ago when I awoke
I saw your grin in a knot of wood
and there was a time I looked out the glass
and saw your face in the leaves on the trees
arranged just so it felt like you were smiling at me.
Then the time I was typing, late at night
and the silly paper clip cartoon on screen
grinned with a wiggle or two reminding me
so much of you it felt for a moment
that your essence was there, animating.
So many times this has happened
I no longer think it strange
but smile and accept that you are still here,
there never was a leaving.

September 1, 2001
Seattle

DAY 246 — NEIGHBORS

Fog horn sounding in the distance
and the purr of an inboard crossing near.
Now a small plane soars across the sky
heading north up the passage to Vancouver Isle.
There must be fog out in the channel
but here a light mist is on the water
that might burn off if it gets hotter.
I'm late for the ferry so I'm first in line,
a paradox in real time.
I'll get to spend a couple quiet hours
watching the sky spinning webs of clouds
hearing dogs sniffing and barking greetings
as numerous tongues speak numerous languages
as children run scattering gulls and crows
as tots toddle the parking lot.
That's how it goes when you're living a circle
no winners or losers, just neighbors.
I'm on my way to Friday Harbor
to see the whales and the clear, clear water
and to sit for a while and absorb the sea
through every pore I have in me.
A journey of no real destination
I travel circumnavigating
the places I love that feed me beauty.
Beyond this there is naught I need get or do.
I drift along like a piece of wood
bumping up against the ferry
or a beach, or a rock, or a coffee shop
all the while feeling pretty good
to be where I am this morning.
It pays to be late, I've a front row seat

on the water and I love wind on my face on deck
but it's great to be sheltered, too.
A sailboat in Sunday sleepiness
is crossing directly in front of us.
The engines have stopped
and the pounding cavitation
as the ferry waits for this sloppy navigation.
Neighbors again, making room for each other,
the ferry being gentle with weekend warriors
trying to navigate tricky waters.
There is no mistaking kindness for weakness
when you are at sea.

September 2, 2001
Anacortes Ferry Parking Lot

ONE RESPONSE

One response to the pain of death
seems to be a concerted attempt to erase
all the evidence—no pictures hung
no mention made, no questions asked of anyone.
Some actually believe this a kindness
fearing any reference might remind us
thinking, "If we can tiptoe around the chasm dividing
surely we'll meet on the other side."
But as avoidance gains ground
the void grows deeper and wider still
till we trip and fall right in
a chasm of misunderstanding.
Then anger begins since the falling hurts
worse than any mention might bring
and that hurt will not leave in the roar of silence
ringing in our ears like tinnitus,
when each lame movement made
to limp around the growing din
is mutely articulated and accentuated
with every slight that ever occurred
over years and years of acquaintance.
Don't let days accumulate,
don't wait years to make a break
from the dysfunction we find
so appallingly familiar
the madness we accept as sane.
Let the pain in till you know what is yours
and what never belonged to you
then sit very still and let it go,
all the pain and hurt,
just let it pass right through.

September 2, 2001
Seattle

THE QUOTA

The sadness, it wrings me out
and leaves me limp and hanging
and my coffee salty tasting.
The remembering, I cannot do it simply.
It's not your picture that I see,
it comes with an encumbering
of all I have lost, your future
and mine as I imagined it.

You found a love and I dreamt you a family
someday distant, after you'd both found
your wings and feet,
dreamt children who would come to visit
and play with toys once loved by you
and I would read them books
and travel once again with Paddle
and carry them on my shoulders
singing of Froggie and Miss Mousie.
I can roll with most that comes
but expectations muddle
if I never dreamed it true
the letting go is no struggle
but your future intertwined in dreams
of what my future would be
and now that you're gone
I do not recognize what is me.

The slate is blank and surely
pregnant with opportunity
but finding the interest and energy to begin
is causing me some trouble.
The cats come and snuggle

and help me with my sadness
and in time I will fill my days
with newfound wholeness
where I'll hold you ever present
and the tears will all be done.
I'm sure of this for you have told me
in countless and unspoken ways
to take the broader view.
I feel you in everything I do
and heard you call, "Mom,"
as I felt your sadness, too,
and I know you love me
and I'll always see you in the moon.

So why do tears come streaming down?
I know what I have to do
and I am trying, mightily
to get along without you.
It's a slow mend after all
as I grow to fit what's needed
and there is, indeed, a quota
though I can't begin to know its measure.
I guess there'll be no hurrying healing
it's just something I'll have to treasure.

September 3, 2001
Seattle

SOMETHING MORE

I wish there was something more.
I found the cat sleeping in your room
on your bed in fact. He looked up at me
with a guilty face as if to say, "Is this okay?"
The door's been closed since you've been gone
I did that purposely to contain your scent
and every day or so and sometimes more
I'd open the door and take a whiff of you
or go and sit on your bed
where I used to sit and read to you
or rub your back and head
till the day came you hurt too much to touch.

Your scent was so strong I kept it in
and kept the cats away
the way you did, fighting dander and
floating cat hair and allergens.
I kept them out with respect for you
and a deep need in me.

This edge I have come up against
this edge of is-ness fills my days
and I wish and want
and the tears stream down
and the cats come and sit
and the laundry spins round
and the birds are singing
and the squirrels stealing apples
but at least someone is eating them.

Weeks ago I opened your door
for a day or two, then shut it again
not ready to change your room in any way

or give your things away.
It's as you left it, simple and spare
for you'd already parted with most
of your possessions.
As I helped you remove the shelving
you told me, "If a person needs a system
like this they have too many things."

And I agreed, believing in you
and in a life unencumbered
by accumulated baggage.
Letting go of the books has been hard
but your leaving has helped me
with the parting, lightening my being
and my approach to living
but still I kept your door closed.
Two days ago I opened it
knowing that as I lose your scent
the cats will move right in.

Life keeps filling space
as it moves through time
though there is one place
that remains quite empty.
I call it empty for want of a word
but it's more a weight than emptiness,
a vacancy,
a longing, aching
that will not go away.
I sit with it and light a candle for you
and wish there was something more.

September 8, 2001
Seattle

GUTTERS

Feeling full of sorrow and all stuffed up
I thought, "Do I have any chocolate?"
But came outside instead, into the sun
to sit a while and feel the day
before I start my weekend's work.
This morning was hard from when I awoke
with tears and sad choking me up
and I hoped a change in scene
might help me get my body back.
Ate breakfast of eggs and toast and fruit
and finishing sat, eyes shut, head back
against the chair, uncomfortable to be sure,
aluminum frame digging into my neck
but I didn't care, I felt so bad
any change felt good.
When I opened my eyes the sky was blue
the kind of blue that you fall up, into
and I noticed something flickering
way up high and thought, "I really am tired."
But it wasn't imaginary spots I saw,
there was something, way up high,
darting about with yellow breasts
drawing me out of my hollowness.
They swooped like swallows
this flock of gold
and were there for only a minute or two
then moving off and heading west
no doubt following the food
they left behind the beauty.
The trees around created a bowl
with me in the center of an ocean of blue

surrounded by pine and fir
and hemlock and walnut
and apples with squirrels and insects, too.
Those fluttering, darting, yellow birds
gave me back my neighborhood
and helped me climb up out of my sad
so I can clean the gutters.

September 8, 2001
Seattle

Alone

This may simply be
my predisposition
but I believe
alone
is the way
we must do many things
and if we never find time
to be alone
the undone
becomes our undoing.

Sorrow grows not
by being alone.
In fact my solitary state
is a gift to me
that gives me space and time
to grieve
and room to breathe
and feel what is real
helping me find my way home

and I am blessed with those
who take me,
caring,
in their arms
welcoming my broken heart
whenever I'm ready
to share.

September 8, 2001
Seattle

Honkers

Winter is coming.
Cold hands and cheeks
sitting on jersey barrier awaiting the bus
accompanied by scarlet flasher
cloaked in darkness
under a starlit canopy.

In the quiet before dawn
I heard a strange mewing
and turned, looking for a cat perhaps
abandoned on the car dealer's lot.
Cocking ears, direction finding
again I discerned the tiny sound
that first caught my attention.

Straining, searching, trying to fit
unknown into familiar
I realized it was no cat, but bird
and rapidly winging toward me.
"A gull?" thought I, scanning sky
but street lights interfered.

Then listening
and shading eyes from lights' obscuring
I saw a slender line strung across the sky
in loose knit "V" formation
swiftly winging, long necks extending
in a southwesterly direction.

The friendly honking was subdued
as only one or two were sounding
and so this flock of fifty, majestic,
strongly muscled birds,

made its way across a stellar sky
sounding very like a kitten.

Sitting sky bottom witness
to this annual procession
my breath in suspension
reminded of the seasons turning
I reached down to extract
my long neglected mittens
from deep inside my backpack.

September 9, 2001
Lake City Bus Stop

TIME TRAVELER

I came by way of the beach, from the south
and saw the ferry dock in the distance
looking glossy and new, all green tinted glass,
beautifully nesting a pedestrian ramp.
Plantings of lupine and myrica,
wild roses and grasses
were comfortably overgrown along side
absorbing every bit of space as they
raucously intertwined.
I quizzically asked the man in the booth,
"How long has this stood?"
and smiling at me he kindly replied,
"For several years in fact!"

In disbelief I turned and gazed
absorbing the days that I've been gone
asleep at the wheel, driven to distraction,
launched Rip Van Winkle through time.
I'm sure it was just a bit ago
we walked here as a family.
None of this existed.
Just a wide open weed patch
graced with builder's mulch
of broken concrete and splintered glass
next to a simple, open-air, ferryboat ramp.
Now here I stand and you are gone
and I don't recognize reality.

September 9, 2001
Edmonds Ferry Terminal

BLUNT INSTRUMENT

Like a blunt instrument,
energy rising to cement
a wall,
protective layer around me.
It does not work.
Deep inside I still hurt
from a pain that has no cure.
Battering ram instinctive way
of getting along in the world
I watched myself and felt the effect
on everyone around me.
Realizing at last
that my protective mechanism
left a swath of destruction behind it.

What is it that I need to protect?
What is it that feels so hurt?
When will I ever learn
that "I" and "me" do not exist
in contradistinction to the rest.
What peace can be found
on this planet earth
will only come when we finally learn
to live in deep love and respect
for our wholeness.

September 13, 2001
Seattle

Book Two

October 2001

The felling of the Twin Towers in New York City wounded me deeply. I noticed myself and many people trying to cover feelings of hurt and fear with a hostile reactivity, which added to my difficulty instead of alleviating it. My reactivity arose with the usual attempts at self-defense, but now I saw myself uncharacteristically going on the offensive. There was nowhere to run where the feelings of loss and pain could not find me and my hitting out at others with caustic anger only made me feel worse.

From my experience losing Colby I knew that I had to be present with my pain and not try to barricade against or run away from it. It was clear to me that I had to hold all that I was feeling close to my heart with great compassion to find healing. It is hard to relate to something so paradoxical as embracing pain to find release from pain. After all, the idea of letting pain in can trigger our deepest fears of dissolution and death. What does it mean, embracing pain to find healing, and how is it done?

Often, when an uncomfortable sensation would occur my habit was to relate it to a past experience that carried a similar feel and immediately begin playing in my mind the tape of that scenario, wrapping the sensations in thought patterns that were familiar. It was a deeply ingrained "knee jerk" habit that so preoccupied my thinking I was unable to clearly see my present circumstances. Anxieties about the future sometimes played a part in this head spin activity but these, too, were unfounded, simply more layers of confusion fueled by my imagination.

Practicing mindfulness—paying attention, on purpose, without judgments—I began to realize that sensations and feelings that accompany loss are not connected to judgments and stories I created trying to rationalize them. The key to healing the pain of loss was to acknowledge all the feelings I had, to breathe into them and deeply experience them while not getting caught dwelling on stories I created about them. When I stayed present with the energies inside me, sometimes awareness of a deeper issue would emerge and other times a difficult feeling would arise, be present inside me for a spell and then simply fade away. Allowing and exploring all the sensations, I was able to gently touch in with things I'd been avoiding when trying to keep my fears at bay, as well as dis-identify with the uncomfortable feelings that occurred. Those feelings were not me and not something I deserved because of something I did or didn't do, they were simply visitors passing through.

The practice of Tonglen, sometimes called sending and receiving, was beneficial when uncomfortable energies visited me, remembering that I wasn't alone in this difficulty. Breathing in the discomfort and then breathing out a healing to everyone who ever shared that feeling, helped me enormously. I found Pema Chodron's book, *Good Medicine*, in which she discusses the history and practice of Tonglen, to be of great value.

Allowing and being present is different from wallowing and rumination. Allowing, or simply noticing, has a lighter touch where I could create some distance from the sensations and explore where they were in my body. Not succumbing to fear or self-recrimination, I could engage my curiosity and move closer to the feelings.

The destructive qualities associated with rumination occurred when I got sucked into a feedback loop of painful thoughts and stuck on a story line treadmill. When caught in rumination, mindfulness practice helped me step off the treadmill sooner than I could have otherwise accomplished.

The act of noticing an uncomfortable sensation without judging it good or bad, deserved or undeserved, made it easier for me to be present with discomfort. In that process I could see that my habit of tightening to fend it off or wrapping it in old scenarios actually increased my discomfort. Getting lost in regrets or anxiety I ended up creating pain from something that had started as a simple sensation. Interestingly, even labeling a sensation as "pain" added a quality of judgment, so I practiced keeping labels neutral, using words like pressure, or tightness, or constricting to describe what I was feeling.

Ruminating on the "why?" or "what if?" was when difficult sensations morphed into suffering for me. Mindfulness practice helped me discern the difference between sensation and story so I could learn to let go of my suffering. The sensations and feelings were still there, but when experienced simply as energy in my body and not an idea, it was something I could more easily tolerate as I noticed them arise, be present in me and eventually dissipate.

Already opened by loss, it was clear to me how vulnerable we all are, no matter how we try to secure our lives. As my heart was broken further open I found enormous compassion for everyone and the outrageous events that occur, compassion for this being human with all our ups and downs, all our pain and heartache. Life/Change/ Death is ever-present and not something that one can hide from.

When holding tight to cherished notions of safety and security that ignore the fact of continual change it is easy to lose sight of the profound beauty of life, present even when life unfolds with difficulty. The truth was, the more I opened to my actual feelings and not something I created with my imagination, the easier it was to bear uncomfortable sensations and the sooner they would pass.

Learning how to open to the enormity of life's beauty as well as pain required my surrendering and letting life pass unobstructed through me. Taking my seat on the cushion, I found strength by simply allowing the exquisite wholeness of all that IS flow through me—the joyous beauty of Colby's life as well as the tragedy of his death. Some equate strength with resistance, but I have found there is another kind of strength in surrender to loss, becoming resilient instead, remembering how a reed that gives way survives the storm that uproots a mature oak.

The Web

We spoke of those gossamer unseen links
that keep us anchored in this place
each one a strand of the web that is us
eternal spider spinning.

Losing love we are cut loose
web torn and blowing on the breeze
the fabric of days ripped beyond belief
as we try to cope with loss.

Attempts to re-weave links to place
emerge from where I left them last
and puzzle me exceedingly,
if energy threads are indeed the source

how do we get so tangled in things?
Boundlessness beyond thinking and dreaming
with strength eclipsing time and space,
no matter which way my body turns

strings of relatedness strummed at each step
sing the song of arriving—
a humming connectivity
deeper than I've ever dreamed
whether waking or sleeping.

October 8, 2001
Seattle

Suspended Animation

Rain is pouring down outside
street gutters, waves
in rapid succession
surging toward leaf-stoppered drains

pelting raindrops on bus-top roof
I sit and contemplate where I am
unable, lately
to discern certain subtleties.

Suspended animation
seems the best I can do
working and trying to live a life
yet not really present inside it

the most lucid moments come as I sit
the rest of the time feigning, a reflexive shutter
opening then closing so rapidly
few can detect

while I seem to be moving
it's not true.
I am a cartoon, inert, still-life creation
utterly unable to engage.

A stillness has descended,
a stopping of activity
awaiting a key to the mystery—
how to resolve my deep grief.

Neither does it leave
nor do thoughts of you
and I feel life suspended
around me.

Days come and go
and I move along
but my heart
is no longer in it.

Like a nursing home resident
worrying her porridge,
lifting spoon, missing mouth,
staring vacantly,

I seem to have
checked out of my body
leaving behind
a facsimile.

Some are fooled by this hobbled pretense,
nodding and waving greetings
but there are those so provoked
by my absence

they angrily try to hammer me back,
a violence so strange in its intensity
I try to reconnect
with little real success.

October 30, 2001
Seattle

November 2001

Just as I was beginning to feel a bit more stabile and able to engage life anew there came another blow, the brutal murder of a dear friend. Hearing this news on November tenth, suddenly I was back at the beginning, stunned, no ground underfoot, unable to be with others, feeling confused and lost. But this time I was consumed by overwhelming anger.

Back to grief's ground zero, complicated by multiple horrific losses, the intensity I felt was hard to bear. I found myself hitting out at others with caustic sarcasm, driving erratically, and generally feeling miserable. The jolt of running two red lights in a row finally shook me awake. I realized that my pain and reactivity had become life-threatening and I needed to find a way to safely discharge the energies I felt.

SEATTLE SENTINEL

A vacancy fills the sky
near the big leaf maple "Seattle Sentinel."
Its sibling we took down weeks ago
fallen victim to a cataclysmic invasion
all rotting and weakened by fungus
swiftly ending this mighty neighbor.
Out on my rounds
scanning sky's perimeter
I can't help but pause at the hole
standing gaping where once the tree stood
and wonder if others will notice this?
Dynamic forces pulling at that spot
mourning and mending the cavity.

November 2, 2001
Walker Ames Estate

DAY 308

This sound of waves brings me cheer
and sea smell, floating past on gentle breeze,
the sun is here and warming so
I touch hand to sand and feel the heat
only on the west facing shelf
cut by last tide's leaving.
Topside is cool and moist below thin crust
November coming fast upon us
hardly a barefoot on the beach
just a couple of wetsuit enthusiasts
and children down the way
up to shorts-clad thighs
splashing, in youthful exuberance.
Marina full of sticks has gone deciduous
and the rolling slope to the east is a glowing,
golden froth of big leaf maple leaves
like curling wave's majestic crest
foaming sunset over top.
Here comes one blissful, barefooted child
way behind her parents
all winter coat draped and zippered up tight
as she strolls the waves softly humming
clad in pink, short sleeved shirt
with jeans rolled up.
Ah youth, clothes can't contain it
as the waves, in honor, nestle her toes
gently loving her abandon.
Here comes a father with child riding high
blue skull-cap and silent regal gaze
as a seagull bobs like a cork over waves
just before they crest, rolling in from the west

and laying down, here, at my feet.
The train behind echoes past
reminding me of your last visit
and words you shared to ease my sadness
for a friend lost to the tracks
the gist of which said we do what we must
and the lingering, clinging,
should be put to rest.
At the time I thought, "Yes,
that's wisdom's reply,"
but sitting here thoughts swirl in my head
bumping up against each other
switching yard full
and no one to guide them.
I'll let the breeze take them
where it will, sitting here still and empty
unburdened by a mind's meandering
blending with the world I feel
gently cradling my being.

November 3, 2001
Shilshole

FALL COLOR

When they don their fall finery
my feet stop mid-step
and stand
soaking in a presence so grand
it seems the first time
ever witnessed.
When did I ever take the chance
to notice them, individuals?
Now arrayed in earth's change
I cannot work past
lost in my everyday
somnambulistic trance.

They grab me by my shoulders
and give me a shake
dusting off my incredulity
that life could be so.
Some, all drama, glowing orange and red,
knit together with browns and greens
to weave a radiant tapestry
alive with luminescent threads
spun of down still tethered
to my deepest self
and there is no other place I need be.

November 3, 2001
Seattle

THE CHICKEN
AND THE EGG

Through visions long ago
I learned reverence
for those who came before,
the pavers of paths
I would have to tread.

Now he who came after
has joined the rest
and the order of existence
that I thought I knew
has been shattered,

rendered
upside down and backwards
as I try to comprehend
the chicken
and the egg.

Slowly
and with gentle persistence
glimmers of wisdom shine on me
and now I see
from a certain point of view

it doesn't matter.
No chicken,
no egg
and all that is left is, simply
reverence.

November 3, 2001
Seattle

TROUBLED

Deeply troubled, it's true,
I can feel a wringing of hands wondering
if needed help is getting through.
But so many do not fit the mold.
Look!
See them falling between cracks I'm inclined
to slip right by, too, puddling
with the misfits around me.

I bear no judgment in this.
As awkward and painful as my truth might be
it's a simple fact
that finding comfort with those who can feel
is vastly more healing
than the shaving of corners
off square-ish pegs
in order to fit in holes round-ish.

This pressure to be just like I was
instead of who I am
may indeed not be coming from you
but all distractions from what is,
these figments of my recent past,
are baggage
dragging heavily,
time now to open to the real.

November 9, 2001
Seattle

Whiplash

I will grow old and you will not.
How many the times I've thought
with comfort
of two old friends navigating and gallivanting
through our elder years,
together if none the wiser.
Always a beauty, held erect
yet how many could suspect
the pain that made you so?
The dignity of your deep strength
in spite of setbacks, many
as you searched for the thread of love
and meaning that could bind your wounds.
And this further wounding, act of taking
and leaving took from those who loved you
everything.
How could this be true?
I am thrown back, whiplash in my grieving
to that beginning absent of reason
flailing, searching for solid ground
that is cruelly not forthcoming.
And your family who number many
so deep in shock there could be no fathoming
the depth of loss still coming,
bearing up, bearing up
brave-hearted every one of them
gathering blood lines under roof
readying, planning, phalanx against the storm
impending.

November 11, 2001
Seattle

MUDRA

Morris Graves said it in paint,
gloved expressions floating, still,
absent of a person to fill, empty
and mirrored here on pavement
in a single abandoned glove
yet strangely animate
holding the pattern of he who wore it
ever seeking that which eludes
reminding me of that deep yearning
prodding, driving, searching for a clue
and seeking, too, I asked the man
residing on street corner
who'd made an offering to the world—
six-bit answers to any query,
"Please tell me the meaning of life."

He prattled on for quite a while
most of it pure gibberish
but in between sounds as he scanned the sky
for words to fill the vacuum
I could feel him struggling and reaching
feel the longing for connection
and somehow in that vacancy
of thirsting, pure and simple
he answered the question that I'd posed
not with his words but in the space that lives,
the void between the lines,
as he strained to fill the unfillable.

November 16, 2001
Seattle

AT SEA IN EASTERN WASHINGTON

Rolling along riding freeway swells and dips
passing solitary farms like distant sailing ships
blinking in and out of view
hidden by rolling waves of wheat
pitching and heaving in the night,
I see a blanketing gray, vaporous sheet
over chasm torn by the mighty Columbia
cresting, curling, splashing over ridge top
as red and white streams of light
glowing ribbons in a sea of black
wind toward a narrowing infinity.
Moon over shoulder is now a high quarter
beaming through fuzzy, gray coverlet
and dusk's last glimmer on distant horizon
is melting into night.
Desert low-riding shoulder artemisia
become beach flora through the dark
rooted in sandy, white volcanic ash
as black gold of buried humic treasure
nurtures a sea of grass.
Roiling volcanic layers emerge
from where the road's wake cuts
showing waves of earth's changing face
while nearby tug of car-to-car
rides an endless magnetic subtlety
suspended across an ocean of time
and cedars stand like bull kelp swaying
in the turbulent ocean of sky.
An ocean of feelings here in my heart
is spilling from my eyes

as I stand on the bottom of life's greatest depths
pondering the distance between life and death
land surfing soils worked by rain and wind
just like the sea uses sand.
In the darkness wheat sways
like ocean-floor eelgrass, blackened strands
layered against a blackened sky,
tumbling in a swirling torrent and I,
sailing toward a distant shore
am at sea in the depths of my mind.

November 20, 2001
I-90 East

Obituary

Our tendency is
to lay down the events
attempting to display a lifetime's contents
on spreadsheet, in brackets
as if we understood.

Our tendency is
to wrap things up
as if somehow done and finished
noting details gathered where paths intersected
where we were for a moment
connected.

Witness to this ritual
I now see more clearly
the essence, lacking substance
cannot be reconstructed.

Physicists postulate alternate realities
and perhaps this holds some truth
for every time we share time and space
our deeply layered universe
can be seen for an instant
a crossroads of different dimensions
as many as there are people.

But standing on the threshold
of Death's bitter taking, here,
at the gate of Rashomon's wisdom
each of us cloaked in disparate visions
we live in dimensions separate,
even distant,

like parallel ports shunting massive amounts
of discretely packaged ingredients
and blind to so much and so many

our longing for connection
ephemeral it seems
too often lived solely in dream
as we weave single strands
through life's infinite unfoldings.

Your time with me
though spanning a lifetime
was more butterfly, alighting then leaving,
the stuff of friendship bridging the gaps
as we went about raising our families.
But I remember the pain, a perennial theme
arising, I guessed, from an absence felt
as you longed for the bliss of a deeper union
once shared with the partner Death took.

So many times an ear for you
I came to know the heartbreak—
to have once tasted the nectar of bliss
the question remained: how to continue
absent of that communing?
And how could there be blame in this,
fed by a culture that feeds the myth—
that there is only one true happiness,
we struggle through days to gain
understanding why it seems
so hard to find it.

The end of line news printed wishful claim
that you were living a life of mythic completion
came as a further shock to me,
reeling from the blow of your brutal leaving,
sheltering words for those left in your wake
which to me seemed cruel in light of the truth,
an affect of social boilerplate.

But you are gone. What harm can it do
if some need to think a lie, true?

My heart and mind recoil from this
wishing you not only greater fulfillment
but an honoring of your deepest truth.

As days go by I am beginning to see,
stuck to the notion that we own validity
is simply clinging to illusion
and anger over words said by a family
grieving and grasping after threads
holds a mirror not to truth but to frustration
at our helplessness in the face of Death.

And I find that while searching for
fantasy mates we miss the ones here,
at Rashomon's gate,
each of us partners in this cosmic unfolding
life's fabric, a weaving of strands, mated
by our simply sharing this time-space web.

And as each of us weaves our version of truth
how can we judge others' absence of insight
when we stand as one at the gates
with no more clue to the meaning of events
than we had at the start of our journey?

While I am certain you have forgiven us,
struggling in your absence,
they with words that naught was amiss
and me, grief rendered sudden pugilist,
standing at the gate of your departure
the choices we face emerge from the mist—
is this portal a means to illuminate
or an illusion propping bolster?

November 21, 2001
Sandpoint

Thanksgiving Dinner

Beautiful turkey and all the trimmings
she sat apart, surrounded by loved ones.
One could tell by looking
with eyes that can see
she'd been hard hit—gaping hole
in her chest standing vacant.

They seemed to make as if
nothing was different
and she wondered how they did it.
"Let's drink a toast to life!" said one,
and she added, "And to death,"
pondering how to blend
with life's giddy avoidance
without going completely numb.

"Let it go, let it go," her mind murmured,
"there is nothing you can do,"
remembering she'd almost made it back,
almost able to engage anew when further loss
hurled her back to pain
and back to the questioning.
She'd asked everyone she knew,
even some she didn't
but none could give an answer's semblance
just annoyingly facile platitudes.

Sitting there poised on the edge of the brink
and grasping for an inkling of the truth
without speaking a word
they could all hear her pain

though no one knew what to do.
From that place a clamor arose
as ripples of energy coursed through the room
out to the stars and maybe further,
crying out for wisdom.
The reply that came was a softening
as those nearby reached out to her
with a gift of such resilient strength—
their love

and an offering to hold her close
while respecting her space in grief
and gradually there came a calming, settling
as she joined them in that place
riding the tide of silence.

November 22, 2001
Sandpoint

DECEMBER 2001 —
JANUARY 2002

Sometimes I was fooled into thinking I was done with some difficulty due to the passage of time or the fact that my thoughts were no longer dwelling on a painful subject. And then, a song or comment or situation would trigger memories and I'd find my body reeling as if the trauma was being lived again.

I found that trauma can linger inside until I open the door to feeling its effect, a process that cannot be hurried. Investigating what was real, deeply entrenched feelings started to come to the surface at which point I could engage them, discover what was true about their source and explore what was needed to promote healing.

The structures I had once identified with, built from my hopes and dreams as well as fears and trepidations, were completely dismantled by my son's death and the tragedies that followed. No longer wedded to the assumptions of my former existence, I was not bound by the "shoulds" and "oughts" that were once a driving force. Ironically, trauma helped to bring my whole being out of hiding into the light of day where I could take a deep breath and feel vibrantly alive without the need to tighten in self-protection.

While truly laid to waste by grief, paradoxically, the place I found myself was as profoundly beautiful as it was filled with pain. And as hard as things were over the first few years. I found my truth preferable to the wasteland of denial and avoidance I perceived all around me. Still, it was a difficult journey, tripping and falling over and over again into pitfalls of clinging, trying to climb off the roller coaster of my imagination.

Finally, realizing that my life was at stake, my commitment to meditation practice was heightened. I found a formal meditation group and resident teacher and took refuge. With the guidance of the teacher, the teachings and the community, I immersed myself as much as I was able in study and practice. I was grateful to be received so generously, even in my time of extreme difficulty, and the discipline of a course of study helped to calm the wild horses inside me.

The experience of losing my son and through his loss, losing and then finding myself was excruciating. Focussing on practice and study, I was gradually able to gain some ground under my feet. It has taken me years of dedicated work to find a path to peace.

Commuters

Something is going on under the dock.
Small black birds are winging in
from the north
toward the ferryboat ramp

and as they fly above the deck
they tumble and swoop
like party confetti,
twisting and turning

and catching the light
till the last possible moment
they pull up tight,
squeezing in amidst the pilings.

I've been here only a minute or two
and as I've been observing
several hundred birds have tucked
themselves into a forest primeval.

This extraordinary migration
may simply be a commuter occasion
finished from a hard day's work
and heading home again.

December 5, 2001
Edmonds Landing

Anger

Sitting at meeting hearing other processes
other prose from other disasters
I kept asking if they'd punched in the nose
those thoughtless, inept, selfish clods
who inevitably step on sorrow's toes.
Twice I asked and twice came the answer, "no"
from those so broken and new to grieving
they could barely address my
cloddish intrusion.

I could never be angry with you.
Having watched you suffer and
realizing your answer
was the best that you could do
my grief limped along unconnected to anger.
Now I simply want to scream,
"Don't mess with me—can't you see
I'm broken!" but the world keeps plowing
roughshod through
unperturbed by my tenuous condition.

At long last having found my anger,
now what do I do?
Discomfort acute with energies misfit
I cast about in fury
needing to ground like a lightning bolt
on any nearby object
but venting brings no real relief
and only makes me sadder
for in its wake the swath of destruction
is growing every wider.

I'm going to have to sit with this
uncomfortable, difficult feeling
without attaching any blame
without needing any answer
just this feeling, that's all I know is true
and if I can sit and be present to
the hunger and hurting and needing
breathing them in and breathing out a healing
there may be hope for me.

December 10, 2001
Seattle

LAYERS OF SIGNIFICANCE

The layers of my existence keep piling on
and at present I seem to be the path
of least resistance.
My teachers say things aren't what they seem,
attachment, the real source of pain
and life's struggle mostly misplaced attention
but the wounding I feel certainly seems to be real
as I stumble and trip over everything.
Tattered and torn and struggling again
this time the cycles of grateful renewal,
that biological process we are visited with
emptiness, confusion, anger, pain
are cycling so fast I can't take a step
without lashing out at somebody.
Finding blame aplenty as if venting could mend
when it only destroys my sanity,
the metaphors of "plus" and "minus"
and all they bring into being

seeming so guilefully real at the start
simply mirror this beginner's bumbling.
Perhaps anger serves to dislodge useless
patterns, getting so blown away
we can then start again but the end-run
blame-game adds fuel to a flame
that is burning me inside out.
Like compost's chemistry
it's hidden from view
and the antsy, jittery careening are proof
I've relinquished the wheel to a child
or an animal that knows no better
than to run from pain
believing the source of it real.
Think I'm getting the message this time
accelerated process abusing mind and body
for I see now anger is like any fix—
another trap to fall into.
Out of control and speeding rapidly
into red lights run and relations traumatic
it's time to rein in my brokenness
to find a quiet place to sit
and seek wise counsel for guidance
for nothing about venting or avoidance
is going to help me heal.
At this point of so much lost
I see there is nothing to win
but mastery over wild horses within
who are driving me to distraction.

December 10, 2001
Seattle

The Stream

The stream running through the parking lot
was four feet wide and growing.
A torrent pouring down
had birds mostly on the ground
when suddenly, on some unspoken cue
flocks would rise in separate groups
and soar tight-knit loops round car and lot
then settle down again.

Looking out my rain-drenched windshield
I saw a crow picking up a bit of stuff
was fully engaged in seagull's dance
of rising then dropping treasure
but it never could quite bring itself
to relinquishing the object
so up it flew then down again
never really letting go.

A juvenile gull sidled up
preempting crow and nosing object
found it unworthy of a gull's indulgence.
"Silly birds," thought I
then remembering my own
thought better of my judgments.

In spite of the storm or maybe because of it
a half-dozen dinghies came round the sea wall
eager for the tossing surf, sailors leapfrogging
side to side, dodging sail, trying to ride
ocean swells like birds ride wind
fully charged from the squall
that appears to be nearing a flood.

December 16, 2001
Shilshole

BROKEN PATTERNS

The patterns of my days
have been further bent
first my son and now my friend
and she, so full of life
with loved ones many
removed from life against her will
mysterious intruder drawing life's blood
with blade, across the rug,
across the floor of the house
that she had built.
The city was in turmoil and nary a soul
remained untouched by this horrific event.
Newscasters twittered like coots seeing eagle
and police like canines searching for a scent
while the nervous flock regrouped
trying to find peace
in a fierce, fierce world.
Sinatra croons my favorite song,
"Have yourself a merry little Christmas,"
the stings and chorus following along
and I notice a line only dimly heard,
"if the fates allow,"
the stuff of life surrounding me
waitresses scurrying
and patrons smiling greetings
while I sit here writing so furiously
this page may ignite under pen.

227

December 20, 2001
Lake City

JAGGED

Jagged, that's how I feel
with energies too big to fit
discomfort acute as I try to exist
casting about like a long-legged insect
legs tentatively reaching, seeking
but finding nothing solid.
Ready to explode, that's how I feel
with angry or sad, I'm not sure which
and at whom? Now there's
a mystery I never will untangle.
The wind was high this afternoon
as I watched a crow, aloft
and struggling, storm buffeted to and fro
as it reached and strained
wings into wind but made no headway
using every ounce of energy
just to hang, suspended.
Succumbing to the gale the crow
turned its head and tumbled from the sky
grabbing for and anchoring on a pole
hunkering down to ride it out
grateful for a port in the storm.
Wisdom keepers help me heal
and find a way to ride this tempest
like a wind-whipped bird
struggling and losing
my circuit breakers must be broken
ante upping and upping I breathe it in
trying to absorb the flow, frantically
searching for a pole to sit.

December 20, 2001
65 Bus

BRIEF ENCOUNTER

Last night as I sat
there came a sudden remembering
just there
it held me in mind and body
wide awake, alert
and deeply interested.
After it passed I could find no trace
for the life of me
no recollection whatsoever
of what it was that felt so familiar
and so good—except the feeling
that for a moment, something
was very right with the world.
Today my sitting practice
sketchy as it is
has a bit more substance
the longing, beckoning finally connecting
my eagerness renewed
another layer of significance
has been deeply woven in.
To the masters this will seem
a trifling incident
but believe me, with wild horses pulling
in a hundred directions
whatever takes me to the mat
is something very good.

December 21, 2001
Seattle

LINE DISCONNECTED

I would like to call my friend
and speak with her a while
but I can't
her line's been disconnected.

I would like to call her people
and speak with them a while
but I can't
their grieving is still a huddle
and my efforts have been denied.

Thrown back onto myself
energy building all the while
discomfort in my body growing in magnitude
I struggle and wonder where
to put this bewildered energy?

Holiday invitations aplenty
interesting movies and food and music
and so many beautiful people
but I just don't fit

and end up seeking solitude.
Guess I'll watch the fire,
take a walk,
then come inside and sit.

December 21, 2001
Seattle

Empty Pages

I had a dream
that I was with my children
and so grateful to be with them
and someone
was it Colby?
was teaching me how
to wash the ink
off all my pages.

It felt good
and somehow deeply knowing
that to wash our pages
empty
is where we all
are going.

December 22, 2001
Seattle

It's Not in Here

I stood in my living room
at a sudden loss and said,
"There's something that I'm looking for,"
and stood a moment in distress,
simply there, a state of emptiness
as I cast about for the thread
of what I was doing, … "Oh yes!"
and reaching for the notebook
went to write a while, attempting to ease
the pressures in my head.

For many years I've struggled
trying to fill inner void
with every food scrap happening by
but it never could be filled.
Similarly afflicted
my friend put a reminder note
on every kitchen cabinet
reading, "It's not in here."

Having tried and failed
to fill the void with people
and continuing to build fantasies
around approaching strangers,
I've finally learned to help myself
by posting an imaginary note
on foreheads saying, "It's not in here, either."

Gardening is the closest I have come
to finding what I'm seeking
with beauty and wonder at every turn
and always gently healing
but I hunger, still, for a connection deeper

such that I've had to admit
the answer to all my searching
is neither garden nor its creatures.

I fill my days with many deeds
earning a living, building community,
full of distracted energies
that draw me away from the deeper need
but once in a while I hit a spot, a vacuum
empty of activities and for a moment I recall,
"There's something that I'm looking for,"
and neither has it body nor flavor nor scent
nor does it crawl or slither or fly or think
nor is it made of ink
and yet, somehow,
it may be all of these.

December 22, 2001
Seattle

FULL MOON

The moon is full behind clouds of silk
that hide nothing, diminish nothing.
As I stood on ferry deck
the shimmering sea went suddenly black
a tanker slipping across our bow
and I recalled Farley Mowat's vision:
two kinds of fog, one encrusted with rivets.
My feet on deck and body on railing
felt the ferry's body straining
as suddenly, behind tanker one came tanker
number two, a blackening slipping into view
fully six stories high would be my guess
and from my point of view
the only indication of its being
was a small square of light at water line
a portal to someone else's world
glimmering, shimmering on the sea
as if that square beam riding the waves
was a midnight sun from a world of angles.
Back home again keeping watch on deck
one year, almost, since he left
the rain is holding itself at bay
in honor of this lunar blessing
while a midnight Jupiter moves closer, too,
zenith in the firmament
and the world around is being bathed
soaking in celestial streams
and neither cats nor I can settle down.

December 29, 2001
Winslow Ferry

ANNIVERSARY — DAY 365

I sought a quiet place by the sea
where I could honor your life
and your leaving
a year gone by this evening.
At first I tried to bring my friends
then realized they could not come here
with me, to this place of memories
but I am not alone — the fire is alive and
crackling and the sea is nearly at my doorstep.
I arrived at sunset in time to greet friends
whose home it is I'm borrowing
and as they left I said to them,
"Thanks for all you've given me."

Shortly thereafter I was joined by the moon
coming up full and clear in the east
as I went to the market for dinner.
Then back to fetch firewood,
searching for the light,
easing down the stairs out into the dark
I went ahead thinking I'd feel my way
just like this whole year has been.
Tentacle feet tapping Braille underneath
I made slow headway till the corner
was reached and there like a beacon
illuminating the stack was the moon
and grinning I laughed, "Thank you!"

Back inside noting hours slipping by
remembering how it went at just this time
every now and then I'd go outside
and monitor the moon crossing the sky
or down to the beach to note tide's exit west
slowly exposing bay flora and fauna
as well as a bevy of rivulets, fresh.

Rising over the house and hill
the moon was gradually swallowed up
by a colossal swirling system that
from where I stood on the edge of the sea
read like a gossamer flower,
veil-like petal-puffs curled and distinct
shielding a star-studded sky,
and for a moment or two it appeared to me
that the moon was the pivot
on which the heavens spun
like a glowing jewel
peering out from the middle
of a cosmic chrysanthemum.
This vision of stars and mist
rose with the moon
and gradually spun itself west
and watching from beach I looked up and said,
"Thanks for all you've given me."

Back inside the hours sped past
as I listened to teaching tapes
those pearls of speech to help me gather
the wisdom of letting go
all the while my inner eye reviewed
a mind-bound video.
When time came to the hour you left
I tried to imagine how it went with you
and sat, this time breathing in your hurt
and mine of that time so full of anguish
in your absence
but my feelings are flowing
like moon's waxing and waning
and with each cycle I am reshaped
and with each dawn new, like you.

So, sitting with a single candle
and noticing how much has changed
I stayed awake as long as I could
there with the candle till it was ash
before I went to bed.
Looking outside I saw the moon hid
obscured by clouds grown very dense,
a blanketing, mending, dropping in meusk
and to the moon and rain, stars and pain
I turned saying, "Thanks,
for all you've given me."

The fire was out as was the tide
and spent from watching wee hours crawling
I went and slept so peacefully
awaking at dawn thinking to review
last year in all words written
but instead am gazing at the bay,
gray from a cloudy, milky mist
transforming distant headlands
into freighters nosing darkly north
while cormorants and gulls are
scouting for breakfast.

Now tide is up and full to brim
and my dawn-lit fire is almost spent.
Am thinking I need to go back home
and start working a neglected garden
but for a few minutes more am going to sit
with a dawning rising from within
pausing a moment to say again,   237
"Thanks for all you've given me."

December 30, 2001
Mutiny Bay, Whidbey Island

WAKING VISION

The cats awoke me
from a deep, deep sleep
and caring for them

opening door to deck
I went searching for the moon
barefooted

and finding, was bathed in light
a perfect fullness moon this night
a year from that you last walked in body.

As it moved across the land
across an ocean of air and trees
across frozen toes and brow

and cloudy breath
a calming followed in its wake
washing sleep from eyes

and tears from chest and I felt
blessed by mystery teaching me
in ways I never could have guessed.

December 31, 2001
Seattle

Colby's Bench

Light rings adorn the waves
puddles of energy caught by the sea
all blue-gray with a silver trim
from sunset over mountains.
Clear sky's a trace framed by ripples of mist
from a blanketing system moving in.
Snow-capped Olympics form a jagged crown
as ferryboat sentries are crossing the Sound
but in truth there is nothing marshal
about them, all creatures mindful
absorbed in their business.

The bay is full of log litter today
dark, horizontal glyphs riding low in the water
seeming hazardous but looking closer I see
birds strung in lines till they submerge
searching for bottom fodder.
I parked down the way a distance
wanting to find what I sought on foot
like the day I walked miles to Stonehenge
a gesture meant in reverence
for the mystery I would meet.
Seagull with a small black crab in its beak
eager juvi by its side, stopped feeding
as I passed, looking anxiously at me
but finally resumed its task.

I'd been told the bench was finished
so I walked and searched
till the last stretch of headlands,
the last stretch of pines and there, indeed,
was a bench draped in plastic,
like you when last we met.
I sat nearby keeping close company
and heard a strolling stranger say,

"I wonder what happened here?"
and almost called out,
"I will never know what happened
but can tell you the story,"
but didn't.
Sitting there feeling protective of the curing
process I saw the cover obscured
but did not hide contents
of a new concrete pad and wooden bench
draped in white translucence.

Colby's bench, here at last
looking toward the mountains west
and up the passage north to the hillside
where your grandma's ashes rest
an exquisite panorama, infinite,
next to the path where you bladed with friends,
yes, this is a fitting tribute.
Unable to resist
lifting sod chunks holding plastic
I saw your plaque was not in place, that space
filled instead by a template, blank.

The setting sun had all creatures restless
trying to glean essence from the fading light
as spinning system's separating strands
deep blue showing behind the gray
revealed the sun behind a cloudy shroud
illuminating twilight.
Lights are coming up around the bay
and the mountains are going black
and I...am packing up and heading home
taking a hint from all that lives,
growing into parting.

January 4, 2002
Alki

February 2002
Looking back at the first
thirteen months after loss

In the beginning my body could barely stand the flow, energy full blown in solar plexus and belly. Then it moved to my heart and head, spinning, churning, opening. Through the top of my head I felt a tremendous current, up, down, I'm not at all sure of the direction. I was a paradox – a full vacancy; completely emptied and yet filled beyond brim with surging energy forcing a quieting, softening, stillness upon me. Old wounds healed instantly, all trespasses forgiven. In a way never before possible I could listen beyond all former impressions, taking others in undirected and unedited and then, completely drained, I would hastily retreat to the quiet of solitude.

For me, time seemed to have stopped and my connection to earth was threadbare and tenuous. The world was spinning way too fast and every fiber of my former existence was stretched beyond its limits. Catapulted to a place where I could barely move, I found my mind was completely blank and body suddenly old and feeble. Every other moment I was forced to gather my derelict wits and consider what were my intentions in this place? Why was I standing by the bathroom sink—was I there to brush my teeth? Of course, that was it! A short while later this process would repeat as I'd find myself standing in the middle of the kitchen. Why am I here? Oh, yes… a cup of tea… .

I'd lost all continuity and with each laborious step nothing could be taken for granted, routine and habits blown away in an instant, that instant Death walked up our doorstep in the form of public servants heavy laden with their tragic news of Colby. Driving I avoided but if circumstances forced it I drove very slowly, gripping the wheel, flummoxed at every intersection, severely challenged by all surrounding and hi-speed inputs. A trip to the grocery was clearly out of the question as the intensity of simple interactions and advertising graphics was enough to blow all my circuits. Besides, I could not begin to think of cooking a meal, in food I'd lost all interest.

Now and then I came upon small flowers oddly in my path, on the stair, in the empty cassette case of a tape that I was playing—a tape I'd used repeatedly never noticing any flora and suddenly it held a single, fresh forsythia flower. Once after an upsetting telephone conversation I rose up quite distracted and returning several minutes later found a small purple straw flower in the middle of the cushion. Flowers like those I'd put on the place he'd ended life, and every time it happened I felt a presence that brought me back to life from the depths of my deep sadness.

Traumatic loss is brutal in its effect but grief can come in many guises whenever our lives meet change, demanding of us a new response to living. And all grieving has a biological process of its own, like old age or adolescence, and if you find yourself in its presence chances are there will be some who cannot join you. Truly wishing to be of help friends and loved ones say, "Call me anytime," and then they're gone. And do I call? Maybe one or two who have always understood me and they always ask, "How you doin?" but trying to explain my state is crazy making for words do not exist to help them see if life has not yet led them on the journey. Like a long distance runner in the middle of a marathon or a molting insect casting an outgrown existence or a solo sailor struggling to survive a storm, I had no energy to spare in bringing them on board.

"Don't tie yourself in knots like this!" he said and I believe his appeal was genuine. I replied, "I'm not tying knots, I'm unraveling them," and thought to myself, "He refuses to feel. Indeed, he comes from a long line of people who have buried their feelings before they were dead." And he was probably thinking that I wear my heart on my sleeve unnecessarily. I could have gotten all bent out of shape by this, taking his comments as an attack at worst and at best, a cold-hearted sentiment. But Death opened a window in me that was so broad the breeze just blew through and I noticed how old wounds, even those I'd once nourished, vanished.

People for whom I had once held resentment came by and I would greet them quietly where I sat, firmly planted. I remember feeling appreciative of their presence, their thoughtfulness in coming. My heart was free, perhaps holding so much pain there was no room left but that wasn't it for the pain had not yet started and I felt truly free of old entrapments. All that energy spent on misunderstandings! Suddenly, I could be with old friends as if at a new beginning, all the while acutely aware of feeling a deep fondness for them and every process, good and bad, that we had ever shared.

Before Death came the understanding that we choose to hold a grudge or not was so highly theoretical I never gave it a second glance, preferring instead to cling to hurts and times of sadness like a pouting child with a broken play toy clings to misery. Imagine how amazed I was to find myself without fear or anger, without space or time tangents, conscious only of fiercely spinning energy hot-wiring me to a new beginning empty of everything I'd ever used to define my reality. The extraordinary openness that I was for a while eventually passed and was replaced by more familiar habits, but a reference point was now implanted like a compass rose anchored to the center of my being, and with it came a knowing that we choose which way we go, toward anger or forgiveness.

Thirteen months have passed since my son's death and I feel a slow healing brewing. I am better. I go to the grocery without elaborate planning and purchase what I want to eat as if I had some interest in it. This is new. Before I had no interest in things, no ability to conceive a thought or follow it through, feeling like a shell with edges indistinct housing only a deep longing that never could be filled and a pain in my heart that was crushing me. Now, from the perspective of some distance as I try to understand my own and others' reactions to this crisis I have arrived at a point where I see there is no way to wrongly grieve. We give life and death whatever we can and it does not hurt me that others are different. There is no need to change to suit another's preference. Each does the best she or he can and whatever understanding grows out of our intentional or inadvertent sharing is a gift. The rest I must do on my own.

I know now very few can help when tragedy walks up your doorstep and I need to be gentle with myself and gentle with everyone else in this place of no real roadmaps. All gratuitous judgments from "How can they be so unfeeling?" to "How can she be so effusive?" need to go, replaced by a little compassion. Everyone wants us to mirror them, to be just like, or mimic some supposed measure of progress but I cannot be other than what I am. Give all the advice in the world it will not help. If you want to help what I truly need is for you to sit with me and listen—nothing to fix, nowhere to else to be— just here with all our feelings.

Healing comes when we share from the heart spreading all of our cards on the table. Some cannot go there with you, who find sitting with another's pain frightening as if they might catch it or worse yet, feel their own which they've spent a lifetime avoiding. I cannot judge them harshly. We do the best we can, all of us, including those ending life prematurely. The point is to be there for each other while letting go of judgments. Since Colby's death I've learned life is more complex than I could have ever dreamed, with layers that are not immediately obvious, rendering superficial judgments not just unhelpful, but downright ludicrous. With this awareness in mind I am trying with all my heart to sweep my path clear of clutter, the chatter pro and con, gratefully accepting what support comes to me and giving back what I can.

There were times when I lamented about the kind of people who change aisles in the grocery when they see you coming. In fact, just last summer at lunch with a friend I spoke to her of my frustration with those who run from sadness saying, "People are afraid of death."

And she told me, "They don't want to hurt you."

I asked, "How could it hurt, speaking of death?"

She said, "By making you remember."

245

So I replied, "How could remembering hurt?"

She answered, "They want you to forget the pain."

I asked, "Why?"

"Because it hurts!" she cried but I could not understand, knowing the pain and memories never leave, and speaking of it, and even the tears were a comfort from where I sat. So she tried again to help me by explaining it from a different tack saying, "It hurts them to see you in pain like it hurt you to see Colby suffering." At last a light dawned and I saw anew the message that he sent,

"There is beauty even in fear and pain but visible only to those deeply submerged in it."

I finally saw and understood my failure towards him, to not be able to stand his pain and instead to fiddle and fuss around it; so difficult for me to witness his trauma standing outside, looking in. I had to be rubbing his back or reading aloud a book, trying with all my might to cure him. Perhaps it's fair to forgive myself, knowing how impossible it would be for any mother to share her child's pain in a manner unattached, but from my present vantage I see it very differently. I'm not looking for cures like those promised by distractions or avoidance, this pain is too deep inside me. Clearly, for what ails me now there is no simple fix.

Humans recoil from pain, even more theirs than yours. We fear it, and cannot be near it, and when we see a loved one in pain, we need to fix it fast. But some pain cannot be fixed and must be lived as it re-works our way of being. In cases like this instead of avoidance a steady listening is needed. There are few who are equipped to handle this, few who can bear another's pain with compassion and loving kindness. They are somehow evolved beyond the rest, perhaps by virtue of pain they've processed but whatever is true about their gifts, I wish for you who are suffering that you may find at least one like them among your caregivers and friends.

And when people wonder aloud if you are "over it yet" I've learned to gently ask if they are "over" the births of their children and grandchildren or "over" their first kiss? All life's events leave their mark, happy or sad, no difference. Look around you! Each of us carries those marks in countenance, mind and body and with every new event or change there is potential for growth toward greater compassion and wisdom if we can let them in. The death of a loved one, or illness, or birth, weaves into our life's fabric in lasting strands that forever color the tapestry that is us.

If you are suffering loss, for whatever reason, seek out others who can share from the heart without judgments or attempts to make your feelings fade. Find solace in those who can acknowledge your grief as part of your wholeness and your wholeness as part of them. When we honor the grief that change brings with it, endeavoring to work through its many layers of sadness—absent of fear, beyond the need to control—only then will we grow into our humanity from a place that is truly whole.

Freeway

My home is a freeway,
cats coming
and going
all day and night long
and my heart is, too,
as feelings ebb and flow
sometimes getting
quite congested
all this traffic in my mind.

February 2, 2002
Seattle

Thin Ice

I understand if you cannot
approach me where I stand

on ice too thin to dance.
What I cannot fathom

is your pirouettes,
the vaulting, spinning

as you speed across ice
the same which holds me fast

approaching a point of breaking.
What riddle of illusion

keeps you in suspense
and how long,

I wonder, will it take
for the message to sink in?

February 8, 2002
Seattle

Not Worthy

I heard the call
and got the message
then felt my body fade
as I squirmed and searched horizon
for a means of some escape.

I cried,
"I am not worthy!"
but the message now imbedded
was not one I could evade.

Struggling with myself
in doubt
searching inner being to find
just what was it
that I lacked

why, "not worthy,"
to be exact
when suddenly it dawned on me
this feeling had no link to worth
in truth I was afraid.

February 8, 2002
Seattle

2:15 A.M.

What is this aching waking me from dream?
Arising from within it seems the gnawing
nibbles at my being tugging heart strings
till full attention is engaged.
Nothing will appease it, nothing
fills the gaping need though I try and try
and try again to stuff it
or avoid it or to go to sleep again.
When it comes my mind spins round
the reasons for its being, thinking this,
or that, the source of so much pain
but if I simply sit with it
unfolding with the feelings,
perceive it deeper than I ever guessed,
broader than my greatest failure
more vast than any sweet success
in fact it's not related to any part of me,
it simply is the state of being
human after all,
this aching is the knowing suffering
lives in good and bad, refuses to discriminate
laced through every happy-sad
enfolding all of life's unfolding
until we find the space to hold it unattached
to meaning or any measure of significance.
Pain is—that's all
there is nothing more to grasp.

February 23, 2002
Seattle

Perhaps

Perhaps it's not an easy thing
standing outside looking in
to fathom how it feels
to have lost a love to suicide.

Perhaps the gnawing grieving
does not clamor at your being
nor can you look and see the battle raging
as raw feelings vie for my attention
asserting reasons for my failing.

Perhaps the sense of utter loss
has never visited your doorstep
nor the lingering doubts suggesting
the one stone left unturned,
the one road never taken,
was the one that could have saved him.

Perhaps the act of sitting
with the pain of never knowing,
loss beyond all measure
bending body under weight

of tear-stained bed sheets
and mornings yawning aching
perhaps the mystery of this living
has not yet opened you.

Perhaps events have yet to peel your heart
or stretch it till it bursts
and you've not yet found yourself
discarded on a lonely shore
with other storm-tossed broken fragments.

Perhaps the juice
that flows across your synapse
is not yet charged with sadness.
Perhaps the gift of your humanity
has not yet dawned on you.

February 23, 2002
Seattle

SPINNING INK

This spinning of ink across a page
from the wool of deepest yearning
this forming of words
from fragments curling
streaming conceptual bridge

this casting of line
into pools of connecting
is driven,
ever driven it seems
by a breath that is being breathed.

February 23, 2002
Seattle

Silky

Not quite suited to this world
this human happening
wild thing residing in your heart
making its way all awkwardness
of silky bound in human body
you would prefer to be adrift
on frigid ocean liquid swift
sleekness playing with the waves
or to drape yourself languidly across
a warming rock to rest.

This humanness craving
softness and companionship
does not suit you,
unaccustomed to comfort
it is not a quality you crave
but to be taken by the longing
as if seized by eagle soaring,
searching,
steady gaze locked on subject
in tune with seasons turning
and all ordinary things deeper,
I suspect it is this
would feed your hunger.

February 28, 2002
Seattle

MARCH — MAY 2002

Mindfulness practice helped me develop courage—the heart to approach difficulty. It does not happen all at once and can take years. Simply sitting with what is true in this moment helps remove all the layers of "shoulds" and "oughts," all the memories of what I did or didn't do and my judgments or sadness concerning those events. From the place of right now I could explore what was happening inside and outside of me, explore strange sensations in a world that was entirely new. Developing patience to simply be present with what was true gave me courage to approach, again and again, the tender underbelly of my vulnerability.

Sitting in meditation, doing mindfulness practice, helped me build strength to consciously approach the truth of my life and from that place of awareness, to engage whatever was necessary for me to foster healing.

I believe this process is an essential part of our growth as human beings. Contrary to our cultural preoccupation with comfort, living a sheltered life free from all difficulty is not a state to be coveted. My most valuable lessons have always come through challenges, forcing me to grow beyond the person I imagined myself to be. Inevitably, hardship in some form comes to everyone. Learning how to work with difficulty made a huge difference in my ability to reengage life after loss.

Awakening

Delicate lace of bare limbs in streetlight
skeletal structure
with new growth emerging
bursting forth in cascading flowers
incandescent glowing colors
against the dark and warming gray of bark.

Look about!
see hillsides turning
ribbons of subtle color
willows wrapped in burning umber
and swaths of ruddy, red alder,
the first to come in spring.

Limbs rousing from their slumber
and like sun's dawning
raw with color
trees alive as you and me,
reaching toward awakening.

March 25, 2002
Seattle

April

The seasons are turning
round again
April is here
bringing snow in the mountains
and this morning my breath
blew away in clouds
like mist rising off the sea.

April 8, 2002
Seattle

Clouds

Water-soaked cotton fluffs inching snail-like
across the sky, humped up high and round
with dark, flattened feet across an invisible density
clouds form a patchwork quilt,
light and dark over desert dry
across slopes ribbed like a sleeping giant's body
articulated muscular strength worked by rain and wind
and clad in polka-dot stretch fabric
of artemisia, sage and lichen.
Every muscle crease is darkened with green
where dew rolls like sweat off hillsides
into the roiling, tumbling Columbia
going to join a salty sea.
Beneath the sensuous rolling hills
exposed by eons of rivers running
are bones of volcanoes layered up
columnar rocky fragments
once liquid and flowing building of hills
in successive molten, blanketing waves
covering all in sheets of rock.
Sitting here watching the clouds snail by
watching a river bent to our will
looking at landforms, weather tilled
I see life as if in an hourglass jar
the flowing erosion of hour to hour
turning mountains to dust and all life to ash
as snail clouds and I go sailing by
shaped by the space in which we stand
molded to fit the air we breathe
being breathed by an endless wind.

April 14, 2002
Columbia River

Phone Call

I get letters addressed to you and grandma, too,
not a terrible inconvenience, these reminders
riding envelopes filling my world with feelings.
And do you know, I still get calls?
Today a voice asked for you and I,
with a twinge of incredulity asked,
"Who is this?…"
a year and four months since you left.
And today down the drive I saw something new,
little dwarf maple, lacy limbs weeping
was covered in newly emerging leaves
dripping life as they unsheathe,
last year, did I miss this?
I don't remember noticing sweetness, newness
busily beginning again, driven by life's urgency
after the stillness of winter.
And look! Blue sky is framing green of trees
and cherry blossoms, as hummer bees
cruise and bumble about my yard.
Had to gingerly pick one up
allowing legs to grasp my glove
so full of spring's exuberance it bumped
into my car so I took it to a rhodi blossom
where legs, searching for solid bottom,
dreamily attached.
I do not remember last year's spring.
How could I have missed it?
Absorbed in grief it simply passed
as I bumbled about my business.

April 18, 2002
Seattle

YELLOW BOWL

I bought it years ago, almost twenty-four in fact,
across the street from the hospital at an
old-fashioned dime store, a yellow plastic bowl.
Unlike most plastic of that time this was thick
and smooth and beautiful, gleaming in the light.
Bowl firm and solid in its weight
and generous of proportions, perfect for holding
fruit nearby as I sat for over a fortnight.
They said they couldn't be sure, indeed, not until
you journeyed back was a diagnosis even possible.
This round there was no chance—
no getting better, no end of pain
no cycling there and back again
your end brought home in brutal impact—life
spilling over no longer held fast
your body an empty container.
I took your meds and filled the bowl
the colors forming a veritable rainbow
and such a fullness! A pharmacist's dream
of health and well-being that never found a match,
then went and flushed them down
feeling close to following after.
Today this kitchen where I stand
has stood sixteen months in your absence
and yellow bowl is filled again
with apples, oranges and bananas
as I sit with where I am, staying steady
with the pain watching the cycles spin and spin
basking in the afternoon heat, eating a piece of fruit.

April 20, 2002
Seattle

*(I later learned that unused meds need to be returned to the police station
or bagged with kitty litter and put in the trash. Some medical facilities
accept old meds. Check in your area for what constitutes best practices.)*

Old

She asked when it was I began to feel "old"
a rhetorical question about life's pain
from one young enough to long for none
and perplexed by the ever growing pain
mounting her youthful body.
I told her, "Old came when I lost my son
and lost my will to live,"
but there was more I could not tell,
more I could not give
for I've learned "old" does not always come with age.
Think of those grinning octogenarians
who are still in love with living.
Indeed, only youth can be very "old"
so old there is a giving up
imagining there is something else,
some other way to feel,
some other place to be
where pain and hardship don't exist.

Aging comes to all who live but "old"
is a wallowing, muddy mind-set
where we allow ourselves to languish.
Seeing this now I know my task
life's journey beckoning as I stand stuck fast
uncertain, frightened and burdened.
But a seed has been implanted from the
mind-stream of luminous wisdom
just like seeded lotus in swamp's deepest muck
from that depth the growing starts
emerging at the surface tranquil,
an exquisite, radiant flower at last.

259

The storyline brings the gnawing grieving
but without that thread it's just my feelings
uncomfortable, difficult to be sure
but something I can deal with.
There is a dawning coming to me
as I pause to grasp deep wisdom
letting go while standing fast
a paradox like all the rest
but this one's reworking my love of life
helping me rejoin the living.
Years may go by as I learn to cope
for nothing on this journey is easy or quick
but now I am quite certain
this way will be my path.

April 20, 2002
Seattle

June — September 2002

We are all ephemeral in this life, imagining ourselves solid, trying to build lives that are concrete and stable. While those imaginary constructs tend to separate, the thing that binds us together is the love we share and the opening of our hearts to difficulty, recognizing that there is no such thing as "other."

Grief made this clear to me when I was broken open and underwent a metamorphosis. Suddenly it was apparent that clinging to a seeming solidity obscured my true nature. Covered by layers of accreted concepts held so dear they seemed truly solid, I actually believed in the imagined self I had created. Unmasked by grief I discovered already inside of me the compassion and love that make us truly human.

As the pain of loss moved through me, I was transformed. Over many months my interior space gradually shifted from a dark and cavernous emptiness to something more familiar. While still spacious, it was neither dark nor frightening anymore. I was moving back into myself, more comfortable with the feeling of emptiness, rebuilding my life on new terms. I began to find meaning once again, moving toward rather than away from pain and with a growing awareness, started to reach out to lend a hand to others in need.

The experience of light that came to me when Colby died made me aware of a Joy writ large that lives inside of me. It is always there, even in the hardest times pointing out the choices I have, to contract in avoidance and fear or open and embrace what is true. In every situation the decision is mine—to move toward anger or forgiveness. Daily, the consequences of those choices were becoming clearer to me. Opening further brought compassion, forgiveness and joy to bear on difficult situations, and contracting simply made things worse. The lessons were continuous, new events where I could see the unfolding of my choices from different perspectives and once again learn the difference between skillful means and stumbling ignorance.

But here again I found the paradox of life, for even my awkward stumbling was proving to be a kind of perfection. Every step I took provided a place of beginning, no right or wrong but simply noticing how I felt and responding as best I could. I was learning that it was enough to explore with sincerity the process of my life's unfolding trying to approach every situation with my best effort and an open heart.

Tears

Standing to honor his son just wed,
raising a cup of joy in toast
I heard this gentle friend proclaim
that he was just "the hardware man,"
all gratitude was due his wife and love
the one who taught them softness.
Reaching for his younger son
who'd asked him, "Why?"
the tears he saw, I heard him trying
to explain the tears that somehow always fall
at every rite of passage,
when even during times of bliss
when joy seems near to crushing us
our cheeks are traced in trails of salt
our eyes brimful with sadness.
So he spoke of birth and hope
and hearts so full of joyful glad
they lift and bubble up
and brimming, spill right over top.

Sitting there it came to me,
"Don't forget the tears of grief
for lives we've lived and all lives lost,"
and thought, perhaps, to raise a toast
to pain and death, despair and loss
by which all brimful hearts are broke
and flood our brimful lives with tears,
love borne through human hardship.
Fearing I might foul the feast I finally stood
and left the place where so much joy had gathered
as tears began to rise in me
a gnawing, soreness welling up,

263

for a love, now dead
and dreams that followed
of what our lives would be.

Later, as I sat to think, "What are these tears,
and what's the link?"
I saw so clearly through the dark
our hopeful, fearful bargaining
imagining we could somehow cleave
cloud from sky and sun from rain,
remove ourselves from suffering
but in these fields of paradox both joy and pain
are born of love and inside each
there is the other
there is no way to separate
what love has cleaved together.

In this living, breathing dream
arising from our greatest sum
a knowing dawns from deep within
that joy and pain are simply one.
Stranger still we come to know
that only broken cuts right through
confusion claiming either/or,
all visions of duality.
When we finally let them be
the tearful seeds we sow in love
will one day blossom, free at last,
made whole through deep compassion.

July 5, 2002
Oakland, California

Stretching

My mind
stretching

across an ocean
of time

eons
of space

has finally found you
here in my heart.

July 13, 2002
Seattle

It's Time

It's time to let you go, I know,
the dream I had, it told me.
Inside the box, fingers sifting through gray,
I grasped your face, a death mask of bone
and wafer thin, like finding chards of porcelain
looking as if you simply slept
eyes closed so peacefully.
What were you doing in that place?

It's time to let you go, I know,
I finally found the strength to open box
and grasp the bag, clear plastic
holding your remains held firmly to my breast
so heavy as I sat, rocking on my zafu.

It's time to let you go, I know,
the men have already left.
I heard them say, "Those ashes are not
truly he — they hold no meaning at all,"
remarks that stunned and flattened me
searching for compassion.

It's time to let you go, I know,
a peaceful letting go at last
ashes scattered on the sea
as compassion finds a home in me
there is no other option.
No matter where I turn in search
the mirror stares right back.

July 28, 2002
Seattle

Can I Possibly?

Can I possibly ever get used to this?
Might as well try walking
on that Mylar seeming sheet
waving dizzily toward me
stretched tight and slightly curved
any walking there would be up
and up, wave top to wave top.

The sun has gone but the sea is lit
by summer evening's twilight
and radiant Venus is rising nearby
as the day is tipping into dark.
The way is somewhere near, I'm sure,
searching will surely find it.

The walkway turned gracefully
round and round, baluster, stair
stepping solidly down
and down they go till they submerge
and down and down my eyes still peer
as if at some lost, ancient artifact,
Atlantis rising from the deep,
as stairs and rail come climbing back.
Nary a soul walks here tonight
perhaps avoiding the lap, lap,
lapping erosion of all we take for real.

August 29, 2002
Alki

Italian Plum

Love's blush on plum
fuzzy, glowing bloom

like an eager heart
leaping from its breast

in greeting
I went to wash it off,

acknowledgment,
and calmly stood there eating.

Every day a dawning comes
one with all the rest,

ageless essence ever present
in everything we see and do

every leaf aflutter
every drop of mist

every heart that's broken
and in breaking is renewed

I feel that fuzzy bloom afresh
heart song in my breast.

September 13, 2002
Seattle

LETTING GO

At first I could not open it,
those ashes in a box,
took a year and a half to find my way
to prying up the hatch
screwdriver free, rendering first glance.
I held them tight these fragments wrapped
up to my breast while rock-a-bye-baby
sitting on the floor I held them for a spell
then gently put them back.

Once opened the box remained ajar
it would not close again
so happenstance has joined them
with my sitting practice
ever opening to gray in clear plastic
as months go flying by.

They stay the same but somehow
I have changed
for fear no longer holds me fast
seeing them now I think of winter nights
hearthside sitting cozily,
fire glowing, burning bright
indeed, those ashes are not he
and I am content with this
only occasionally wondering
how long it will be till ashes
find their way to the sea.

September 15, 2002
Seattle

Dizzy

Awoke this morning dizzy,
dizzy,
one foot, two feet planted firmly
trying to cross the floor
I felt in imminent danger
of crashing into walls.
Reeling head spin
hoped sitting would surely settle me
and it did, somewhat
but when I arose
the world was spinning,
spinning,
dancing me on toes
so much I dared not ride my bike
but drove
and bus stop waiting saw the stars,
Orion in his usual pose,
as the world was turning,
turning,
spinning me
and setting moon in full regalia
gracing all with luminosity
it dawned on me,
"What is this place I call my home?
How do I rise and greet each morn?"
spinning, spinning daily threads
following glowing tracings
that mimic something solid.

September 20, 2002
Seattle

PAINTING

For its warmth I choose the darkened red
a radical departure from my usual crisp white
then noticed it splashed across
late summer sunsets
and fall's passion
painting Liquidambar limbs.

The red we share no matter our color
the red of love and that of anger
and too, my teacher's robes
simple and sacred
indeed, the shade of blood.

Radiant pigment
reminder of impermanence
taken to heart
as I lean against an absence,
the opposing white wall,
carefully cutting in
the edge.

September 22, 2002
Seattle

SOLACE

The log was shaped
like an arm curved round my shoulder
or a sleeping,
spooning torso
but these comforts
do not draw.

It is the sea that beckons me
to breathe,
to join the whistling wind
and wander with wave's booming echo
rolling slowly down the beach,
to revel in the rankness of rotting kelp,
steep in the sweet scent of salt.

Like a wild creature's deepest instinct,
a wayward, wounded mammal
this is the only way to help
when feeling lost and frantic.
Whenever I cannot find my way
my feet gather me up
and bring me here,
this place, my only solace.

September 27, 2002
Alki

WAVES

Have you ever noticed
waves always greet shore
at an angle?
No matter the twists
and turns of beach
at any place along the line
the meeting will be oblique
slipping in between the troughs
the forces never squared at ninety.

No matter where you are,
what state you're in
somewhere deep
our bodies know
while thinking mind lingers
round the bend,
yet to feel the impact.

It's a kindness when in trauma
this distance that we keep
imagining ourselves separate
while wave upon wave
washes our shores
and minds are left to grieve
our bodies slowly work it through,
the knowing held within.

September 27, 2002
Alki

SHADOW PLAYER

Shadow player in a puppet world
city dweller seeking the sea
I come here occasionally.
No one sees me,
a passing stranger,
casually surveying the beach
while sitting crone-like on a bench
hunched over my notebook's
curled-finger scrawl.

Beach fires reflecting on gathering faces
serious walkers striding briskly by
bladers' and bikers' bodies toiling
meandering strollers and I—not unfriendly
this distance, just anonymous
under street lights
as planes overhead roar
on their way to a runway.

Shadow players, all
as we craft our dramas
playing them out over pages with lines
moving in rhythm, moving in rhyme
drifting through space
like tide drawn beach bottles
breathing the ebbing
and flowing of time.

September 27, 2002
Alki

MIDWIFE

Something is coming.
The air around me is pregnant
and the sea is crashing expectantly
swollen curves carrying
each wave to shore
umbilical cord cloud
curling off at horizon.

Like a midwife
I'm waiting
on something
I know not what
hoping it will arrive shortly
like the moon
through soft folds of cloud
a natural birth,
straightforward.

I sit
an eager readiness
as beach pebbles hum
a restless tune.

September 27, 2002
Alki

November - December 2002

My body awareness is usually way ahead of my thinking mind. At times I get the squirrelly jagged jitters and wonder, "What is this feeling?" until remembering that a significant date is approaching. As the years have passed I have learned the importance of honoring my body awareness as well as anniversaries, making sure to have a plan, however simple, on Colby's birth and death days. This helps me bear the tumultuous energies that sometimes emerge around those dates. I never know which it will be, a harder or easier year, but having a plan in place is always helpful.

It can seem that after a person dies their existence simply falls off the map of life but for many survivors, anniversaries remain important.

Claws

Claws on street in swirling circles
halting, jerky skittering
scurrying, leap frogging
cartwheeling by

stuttering motion catches eye
alerting and alarming me
as if driving a road
chock full of crabs and frogs.

But it's only oak and maple leaves
like curled and painted parchment
blown dry after the morning rain
by swiftly passing cars.

The sky is dark and thickly looms
a heaviness shifting and slipping such
that last light seems at first to leer
then gently smile at me.

But it's only storm clouds moving past
clearing paths for moonbeams
as I note the signs and make a story
that somehow reads to me.

November 8, 2002
Lake City

SQUIRRELLY AGAIN

What is it that I'm feeling?
Jagged and squirrelly and reeling
I seem to have once again
lost my way.
The rains have finally come back through
and perhaps memory's body
is recalling
what it was to have newly lost you.
The distance to my nearest neighbor
might be an eternity,
rain pelting loudly on my roof
fir needles stopping up all the drains.

There is no fix to this
but sitting very quietly I find some relief
some semblance of serenity
letting go the story, letting go the grief,
letting go the anger that would destroy me.
Sitting and sitting and taking it in — rain
and sirens and distant friends.
Letting it be just as it is
with some measured dregs of sanity
amidst a whirling ship at sea
going down all around me.

November 16, 2002
Seattle

Part Knows

Part knows his leaving served me,
stands simply in acknowledgment
of the gift come through the door
that cataclysmic opening
to compassion deeper
than I could have ever known.

And then comes the crushing
when stilled by the loss of a son
waves of grief roll over me
tossing, tumbling, rendering
a flotsam jumble of flesh and bones
soaking in a salty sea
of loss born of remembering.

So back and forth I lurch along
an awkward, struggling human being
making my way through laughter and tears
and the sharing we do as we gather years
no up, no down, no here and gone
weaving all into a fabric, living
that looks like you and me.

You ask me how I do it, how find
the joy within the pain and I say to you
from where I sit there is no loss, there is
no gain, just the sharing of our humanity.

November 25, 2002
Seattle

WHERE ARE YOU WITH IT?

She asked, "Where are you with it?"
and I tried to answer honestly
with words that might explain
but couldn't
for I felt in her query
a barricade
halting attempt
to shield her from the pain
and somehow keep it distant.

Not in words but there,
palpably, in her fear
bracing against the intensity of loss
so many shy away from
that is now my hearth and home.

I have come to know
he is always near
as sadness ebbs and flows
and I find my way
through life's broad tidal washes
sitting, walking,
on the path
to deepening compassion.

December 3, 2002
Seattle

CREDENTIALS?

Indeed, one might ask
what right have I
to assert myself
what layering on
of education

and experience
could possibly
give me the temerity
to post these words upon a page
and ask that others share them?

And I could make a list,
the ivy league schools, those degrees
of singularity, that verity
many take as proof of worth
but I'll tell you now how it seems to me.

For all the living years gone by
the piling up of things and deeds
layering on incessantly
promises of safety
and security

it was not until the day
there came to me a stripping away,
a peeling, coring,
laying bare and opened
that true worth dawned on me.

December 21, 2002
Seattle

Book Three

2003

Following the natural path of my grief, realizing there was no other place I needed to be, allowed my life to unfold in a manner I could fully embrace with both mind and body. There is a readiness factor to this process. Everyone is on their own schedule, with an awareness that is perfect for their particular needs and development. Trying to rush toward a desired goal rarely gives the desired effect. Rather, life is an unfolding that, as John Lennon said, "happens while you are making other plans." Wanting pain to go away is a perfectly natural human response but pain is not resolved by wishing and wanting. Instead of trying to avoid, which brings no relief, I learned to move toward, slowly, gently and in small increments.

Try this yourself. Notice what you are feeling in your body and mind. Experience the sensations and sit with them. What happens? Does the pain move or change? Letting go the storyline is key to climbing out of one's misery. When pain is too much, focus on some part of your body that is ok, taking attention off the point of greatest anguish. Then come back and see if there is any change, any subtle shift in the sensations that are occurring. Take a walk, make a cup of tea, write a poem, call a friend and when you are able, take your seat again. Try to follow the thread of sensation and see where it leads. Healing is a slow and gentle process, neither forcing, nor avoiding.

Distractions can be of help if discomfort is too great but ultimately I could not distract myself away from deep grief and pain. There was a working out that had to be done, that could only be accomplished by gently approaching rather than avoiding.

Mindfulness practices, which originated in Buddhist teachings, were the greatest help for my healing process. One need not be a Buddhist to practice mindfulness for there are many centers nowadays that give instruction without any reference to a particular philosophy. If you are curious, find a situation that suits your needs and ask questions as they arise. The benefit of mindfulness comes from doing the practices and finding a community that can offer some guidance. That community might be in books or on-line teachings or it could be with a group of people in the neighborhood. Mindfulness is not an intellectual or faith-based endeavor and need not threaten one's deeply held beliefs. Find practices you are comfortable with and make space in your busy life to do them.

Also essential for my well-being over the years has been the community of loss survivors. Seeking the company of people who are able to relate to my experience has been essential. Many survivors have engaged outreach of one sort or another as a vehicle for healing and our community is becoming an effective change agent. Accepting that I cannot alter what is past, I, like many, have focussed my energy on alleviating the epidemic of suicide. We are working to raise awareness as well as improve pre- and postvention efforts, sharing our experience to inform and help others.

If you wish to help a trauma survivor, consider that you are not there to make them feel better, they are not going to feel better for a long while. Visit to support them in their grieving process. Do everything you would do in the case of an illness or death by another cause, no difference. Sit with them and listen to whatever the survivor has to say. Ask about their loved one. Try to leave your judgments elsewhere. These are things that helped me.

If you are visiting and silence happens, hold the silence as sacred space and wait for the survivor to speak. When you feel you may explode with anxiety if the silence goes on any longer, breathe deeply into that feeling and remain silent. Giving survivors the chance to speak their truth is vital, without any editorializing by others. If you feel fear, acknowledge that feeling and ask the survivor to be patient with you as you learn how to best respond to their altered reality.

Do your best to be truly present during your visit and try to stay attentive for a lot longer than you imagine it will take for the survivor to heal. The idea that a survivor will ever "get over it" is confused thinking. We eventually learn to how to weave loss into our lives but it does not go away and the people who accompany us as we make our way through the labyrinth are a treasure.

IF ONLY

Even now, two years gone by
I sit and ponder how
and why
and conjure up, "If only."

If only I had stopped mid-track
and ventured further in our search
if only I had taken him
to the ends of the earth
and back

if only I had lost the cats
sold it all
every shingle and stick
and steered my little family
to a place far away
from trouble.

If only…

And then I come to where
I see
the dream amidst reality,
grabbing the reins
of lives I've loved
to steer them
somehow
safely home.

February 6, 2003
Seattle

WHAT DOES IT MEAN?

Why do we say committed suicide?
I mean, why not say she committed love
or he committed laughter?
Words uttered from mouths removed
having never tasted it
wreck a curious kind of havoc
in the heart of many survivors.
And the breach that causes such offense
along with the need to stigmatize
is it not more insult to our vanity,
more reminder of our frailty
than offense to humanity?

To die of affliction like any ailing body
tattered, torn, on the brink
beyond finding any link
so wracked with pain no option remains but we
in horror that life could so test
and terrified of who might be next
shrink away, heaping judgments
on all who've left crossing a border, taboo.
And I ask you when does one "commit" the act?
Just how do we read the walking dead
turning away from the fullness of longing
that signifies a life?
And how to view the random stuffing,
heady diversions, walls we build around our hearts,
these various numbings we engage
hoping to soften the edge of pain
that *is* the human condition.

February 16, 2003
Seattle

MORE THAN THIS

More than this,
(or is it less?)
I daub eyes with bed sheet
and turn
waiting for it to pass,
the wave that just swept through.

One could read it as sadness
I often do
maybe with a twinge of anger
or maybe simply pain

but it's more than this,
no matter how I look
it's more
more than all the feelings
I could ever find a name for
larger, fuller
more real.

Trying to fit this into logic
the numbers don't add up
this place where words
and feelings shed away
as well as what I pine for.

February 26, 2003
Seattle

JAMMIES

You have become part of us
like yesterday's laundry
worn thin, comfortable
ever-present.
You hang about me in the jammies
I've taken to wear
soft, brown-plaid flannel
the elastic in the leg
binds a little
at my ankle.

And your brother, too,
is wearing you.
I saw your thread-bare
boxers in the laundry
when he came home from school.
Not a word was spoken,
there was no need to.

February 26, 2003
Seattle

Nothing Quite So Real

There is nothing quite so real
as the day Death climbs your stair.
Left broken, some feign healing
become rigid like trees
building callous wood,
walling from without
barricade cells partitioning.
Alas, not made of cellulose
the calluses we build
neither hide nor heal.

There is nothing quite so real
as taking in what simply is.
It is a ruptured opening
accosting and enfolding you
till suddenly your love is there
in every leaf and twig
there in flower, pebble, puddle, riddle,
in every moon and starlit sky
there in sunlit seas.

I sit and write to you, dear friend
I sit and write to them,
our children, lost along the way
there is so much more I want to say
but silence draws me close again
and I bow to that within.

June 25, 2003
Seattle

When Things Are Put

When things are put
in motion
who can say
what it is
that moves
or where we are going?
As we move deeper
into our hearts
the journey simply beckons.

December 3, 2003
Seattle

360° of Perfection

Nowadays seems I can almost feel
sudden pebble dropping down
and just as suddenly, life softly folds
and knits without a sound
the torn fullness,
reverberations rolling 360° out
and into.

I cannot explain the event.
Cannot draw across time and space
to show how a pebble dropping
leaves its mark on pond,
the ground,

every particle, every molecule
instantaneously altered
utterly changed by the light
touch of pebble passing.
Faster than light the effect.

The surface itself heals the event
like callous wood builds a swollen filling in
and just like water heals each torn place
something registers every shift
and is simply, wholly
different.

Like a mighty maple
bending under its own weight
the hidden, fractured places
are perfectly contained
a wholeness that remains
perfectly changed and broken;
perfectly imperfect.

Woodworkers know this.
Hammer-headed carver hears
the hollow, wasted sound
seeking succor, seeking shelter
finds those perfect imperfections
beautiful.

December 25, 2003
Seattle

Worry Wave

Dry today, and bitter cold
walking over darkened streets
the way was gilded glitter
all available moisture having gathered in crystals
so heavy in spots they almost seemed
to rise in flurries blinding me.
Star studded heavens adrift overhead
and wind bruised, frozen cheeks
hardened by my set of jaw
bracing to withstand the chill
I followed behind a shadow,
a form that so resembled me
I thought to stop and look but didn't —
heart gone out and light gone with it.
Instead I turned to board the bus
and riding, felt an urgency,
a silent pressing from within
pushing against my wall of chest
accompanied by a franticness
that began to be alarming.
"Coming unglued, coming unglued,"
my voice, in panic, chanted.
Now I see it differently
taking time to sit a bit, making time to simply be
I find this simple remedy:
drop the story, embrace the pain,
is how to ride a worry wave
once it's put in motion.

295

December 29, 2003
Seattle

2004 — 2007

The spiral that is healing often brought me back to difficult feelings but each time with a bit larger perspective, making loss a little bit easier to bear. Trusting my own unique approach to a process that many have undergone was essential. Each of us has something to offer and each person's offering is one piece of the puzzle, important for bringing the whole picture of humankind into focus. Like the pebble leaving its mark, however small a contribution we bring, it creates a ripple effect that may help others in ways we will never know and could not have guessed.

Times when I've felt stuck, there has seemed to be an inner working out taking place deep inside, below consciousness. This working through cannot be pin-pointed exactly so I have had to surrender and trust the process, allowing healing to take shape inside of me. As always, the paradox of life is present here, too, in that it has taken both a relaxed allowing as well as my concerted effort to foster healing.

Loss helped me gain a new perspective, showing me how issues can be resolved when seen from a different point of view, where apparently conflicting elements became simply part of a larger whole. My perplexity with the world of dual and its myriad seemingly opposite components was resolved when I discovered the oneness that encompasses every aspect of being. Suddenly, differences were no longer in opposition, but were simply part of what life IS, full of complexity that confounded my imagination and stretched my understanding. As my awareness grew, conflicts that once seemed to stretch me too far, began to open me to a broader way of seeing and being. Now, no matter from what perspective I look at it, I see that life is never either/or, but always both/and.

As yet, I have found no end to this process, no arrival where change, grief and growth are finished, for new challenges arrive daily. Seeing my entire life as a meditation, taking mindfulness practice beyond the cushion, has helped me move away from old, mesmerizing and entrapping tape loop story lines. This practice requires my full attention and makes me laugh when I trip over the most obvious hurdle. When I experience a familiar knee-jerk reaction I try to remember to observe rather than act on impulse and so doing can sometimes create enough space to reconsider my habitual patterns and be more appropriate in my response to whatever is arising. Having compassion for myself as I trip, over and over again, doing the best I can.

To find release from the pain of loss I had to go the distance and do the hard work of discovery. I believe there is no more important work, nothing of greater consequence for our lives. My former life and what once seemed "real" to me ended with my son's traumatic death—a tragedy of immense proportions that set in motion a gift of awareness helping me not only survive but grow. Mindfulness, a simple though not easy practice, has helped me find a path of recovery after trauma, find new meaning in life and ultimately, redirect my life's efforts toward service.

ALKI MEMORIAL

I was on my hands and knees
Brasso and rags and a bottle of water
polishing salt spray from the marker.
"That is so nice, what you're doing,"
came a robust, smiling voice,
"did you know…?"
and hearing my reply
the stranger startled, lost his mooring
and drifting, gazed off in the distance,
knit his brow slightly
as if my words were square pegs
he could not fit into the roundness of his body.
From somewhere far away in disbelief
he murmured, "…we were just with…"

The sea is rough.
Waves crash against and splash over top
catching behind the walled embankment
gathering in a depression,
a sunken trail worn by many feet
where sea water gathers in puddles.
The hawthorn is getting a salty drench.
Gnarled and twisted top
branches intertwined and laying against
eventually to knit as one
leans into the wind and I into it
bracing against the cold of winter.

January 2, 2004
Alki

In Dream

Sometimes it happens this way
in dream
as the ground fractures,
gives way, slips down,
a hand reaches out and grasps ours.
In that moment of utter despair
losing everything
there is no recognition of a face
just a sudden, firm grip
pulling you back from the abyss.
And so it goes
as we live our lives in dream
we fail to see the one
who reaches out their hand,
who grasps ours in a gesture life-saving.
Years ago it was I saw this,
felt the earth give way and watched
as the ground I stood upon melted
with me perched on the edge, going down.
In dream I saw a hand extend
and grasp mine, pulling me back to solidity.
Over and over again I saw myself
plucked from the moment of destruction.
I did not know then that it was now
nor did I know it was you.

2004
Seattle

Natural Disaster

When the earth moves
like an ocean
the seeming solid
liquifies,
ancient gnarled giants ripple
like saplings in the wind
and asphalt streets suddenly
undulate,
satin ribbons.

When tears move
like an ocean
wind whipped and swollen
pounding on shoreline
breeze building
on dark clouds of emotion
unstoppered by grief
down comes the torrent
across page
after page.

March 12, 2004
Seattle

Velcro Patches

I leaned against the wall
scant nails peeling, trying to get an edge
as part of me said, "I cannot do this."
Two black, rectangular Velcro patches
about the size of a pack of matches
stuck with such tenacity
as my fingers strained to pull them free
(part of me that knew I must)
the sheetrock tore off, too.
Fully bonded, that's for sure.
A simple fix will mend it: spackle,
then sanding and a little paint
will have it seeming good as new.

That's all we need it's often said,
"Cover it up and paint it done,"
but the house of my body, broken through,
does not respond like wallboard.
I've tried it all along the path
tears and friends and chocolate patch
to fill a hole that is there still,
it never could be filled.

Now at peace in the midst of struggle
I'm taking a different tack.
The doctor tore the scab off, too,
he seemed to know it did not serve
the healing that was coming through.

March 25, 2004
Seattle

NOT OTHER

There is no other thing we need do
but give the gift of ourselves
to each other.
There is no other place we need be
but in this present moment.
Love is here
soaked through every grain of sand
permeating every surging wave
the log on which I sit
the coffee warming hand and cheek
waiting for my messenger moon.

Love is here,
there is nothing other.

The patterns across the beach
of wind and sandy feet
sky, azure blue fading to burnt sienna
where it hugs the sun's retreat
mountain ridges, stars above
I know you
and breeze, filled with the scent of salt,
chill edging in as night descends
while every inch and ounce of me
radiates warmth of loving all I see
one with me
not other.

October 13, 2004
Alki

NEVER A LACK

I did not have daughters, I had sons.
Would watch the little ones at the park,
pretty pastel leggings with frilly skirt add-ons,
and marvel that finally girls
could slip down hot summer slides
without burning their bums.
Don't get me wrong, I felt no lack
in fact, my preference has always been
tees and jeans, the sweet rough
and tumble of two little boys suited me.
Whether cleaning the roof or learning how to iron
my boys got to see me being father and mother
while I watched and marveled
as friends raised their daughters,
how different, but never a lack.
The fathering I did from a distance
my necessary effort inadequate to the task
and they reminded me every time I held back
unready to plunge into fool's play
crossing ice flows where water coursed beneath.
I got to learn both sides up and down
and found in time the mystery revealed:
all of it a mask, the roles we play.
Besides, each side of dual has it's gift to teach,
its toil and unrequited longing
and in the process of discovery
I learned to offer my hand in peace and say
from my heart, "Different, but never a lack."

December 8, 2004
Seattle

Edges

We wonder about our edges
wonder and speculate
playing off fears and fantasies
saying, "What if…?"
never realizing that the day may come
when our world fabric splits
and the stuff of myth
steps out of the void.

The night so long ago,
wanting to acknowledge him,
hurting from mysterious pain,
the watcher in me stood her ground
while mystified, baseless,
saw my body walk away.
Twice it occurred in rapid succession
and no matter my imploring
those feet could not be turned or swayed.
Thus a witness, bodiless,
I missed his parting.

Could this happen?
It did.
And now I find myself questioning
that which I've always taken
as substantial and essential,
having experienced a split
so full of consequence.

December 8, 2004
Seattle

RECOGNIZING

Could there be anything
more perfect
than the dawning
arising from our own hearts,
the light shining out
from within?

When suddenly
a friend's eyes
are lit
with a radiance
we recognize
as kin.

December 15, 2004
Seattle

MOON MAGNET

Last night
the moon magnet came
and drew me out
from under my covers
pulled
the very heart of me
out from under
layers of dusty
remembering
to lie simply
basking in radiance
past polarity.

305

December 27, 2004
Seattle

There is an Ocean

There is an ocean
residing in my heart
of unfathomable depth
and broad beyond horizon
it rests there.

Sometimes when joy moves
the sea swells
and spills upon the shore
tears for a presence felt
an absence,
an unfinished story
lingering on the shifting sands
of my imagination.

January 28, 2005
Seattle

THE HEART'S JOURNEY
— IN PRAISE OF TEARS

Finding an empty heart
empty even of the frosty breath
of a brisk winter's chill
take that stillness
and let it be the container
into which joy will flow
like the tide as it turns,
the fullness of tears
spilling into the vacancy.

Finding you cannot stand
let your heart Braille its way
blind and lost
follow the scent of salt
one foot in front of the other
let your feet take you
to that place
where the wind is making
an offering
and lean into it
as you would lean
on a friend.

February 16, 2005
Seattle

Despair

Despair lives in my breast,
my belly.
Usually quiet
for some unknown reason
tonight it began to clamor about
driving me this way and that
but the place I sought
eluded me.

Ready to burst I headed west
desperate for a sunset,
desperate for dancing waves
and rainbow hues of
cloud reflections,
clickety-clack upon the tracks,
mountains draped in misty wraps,
desperate for the smell of the sea
floating on the wind.

Ah, squirrelly is here again.

March 6, 2005
Seattle

Marrow Spring

They ask, "Why do you have to go
so near the edge?
Come back to our comfort zone,
do not wake what slumbers
with your tears."

They cannot see
from where I sit

familiar landscapes
instantly erased
leaving me perched
on an edge I am growing
accustomed to.
Creature comforts, chaff
blown on the wind,
edge honing me
to a boney essence,
warm tears welling up
from the marrow spring.

September 8, 2005
Seattle

COMMUTER IN THIS PLACE

Commuter in this place
called life
what care I of traffic!
Lament the lack
of movement
if you will
but can you be
still
uncertainty building
in your belly
holding difficulty
as if it were
the beloved?

September 8, 2005
Seattle

Clear Spring

From her being there flows
a steady spring
body forming the edges

of a clear pool
water-line reaching
right to brim.

She can see herself
and everything
reflected there.

When wind rises, fire leaps
or earth grows unsteady
there comes

an overflowing
out-pouring of liquid
some mistake for sadness.

It is not so.
When energy moves
water spills.

September 10, 2005
Seattle

LOOSEN

Leave those old worn out
boots at the door
the ones you've been wearing
uncomfortable, ill-fitting.

Leave your wrap there, too,
that one binding you so,
the whispered,
"Not good enough."

Let your feet dance bare about the room
as the winds of your soul
loosen the flood-gates, a heart-burst
of singing your praises!

Oh, blessed one
sit with us here,
safe
amidst all our imperfections.

January 13, 2006
Seattle

Death Came and Undressed Her

Death came and undressed her.
I could see this clearly
vulnerability,
awkwardness,
trying to pull on old masks
that no longer fit
to somehow find a way to present
a persona made ash
through grief.

And hadn't I
just a moment before
asked for strength
to hold all gently
despite the deceptions
the guarded expressions
not quite covering
and suddenly felt my own heart
snapping shut
in the presence
of so much pain.

February 6, 2006
Seattle

CURRICULUM VITAE

It is love that threads
the pages of our lives
into one readable volume.

Love alone binds together
the happenstance, the painful,
the coming undone.

Love sails around and through
the winged fortress of our years
flighty, unruly, seeming solid.

And here we stand on the threshold
present, still,
full with recognition

the beating heart in our breasts
is not a separate thing.
Not separate at all.

February 10, 2006
Seattle

EVEN HERE

Even here,
in the heart of spring
a misty morning can find
moisture swelling on leaf tips.

Even here,
at this forested enclosure
edge of a clear, still pool
comes the up-welling.

And after a while we begin
to comprehend
the ocean heaving
loss knitting, wave upon wave
into the fabric of our being
every strand and fiber
like salt brine, lifted,
carried by the breeze
and out of the fog
comes a healing,
a knowing,
we are not alone.
Indeed, never have been.

April 29, 2006
Seattle

Stillness Can Be

Stillness can be confused
with lethargy
activity with healing.
Shaking loose is not the key
arriving at some "other" me
take lessons from the humble larva
let go the gizmos,
mental gymnastics,
the putrefaction of misplaced anger
try calming, quieting,
holding inner flow tenderly,
once seeming difficult
come to *see*,
take nourishment from the darkest torment
like seed basking in sun and rain
awaiting the moment
of deliverance from self
into the wholeness of being.

April, 2006
Seattle

Ruined

Ruined by loss
she could no longer
tread amidst
eddies of gossip
swirling round her.

Ruined,
she could not share
bitter slights and provocations,
no grudge left to hold to
she sank
in an ocean of knowing
there is more, so much more
below the cream
we are craving.

Ruined,
indulgences sweet
no longer served,
soured in her mouth
as the winnowing longing
whispered
go deeper.

May 23, 2006
Seattle

READY

I am standing at the
threshold of your leaving
a door you passed through
years before
and still I stand here
grieving.

Every evening I sit
under the setting sun
like a seed in the sand
awaiting germination

eager to feel
the bursting of chaff
in cotyledon's
transformed arising.

May 25, 2006
Seattle

WHO COULD HAVE GUESSED?

The flower never did
as it dwelt amidst
the pea patch.
And then one day
light streaming
essence of its being
unfurled from within
an opening
come into its own
surprising revelation
rain soaked
sunlight bee
crawled right in
treading tenderly
nectar sipping
as sounds of celebration
resounded
throughout the world.

June 23, 2006
Seattle

FIRE

The fire is here
inside
like dawn's slow spread
over heart's horizon
once a conflagration
engulfing every fiber
of my body,
wild fire
consuming the dry tender
of my early years,
now is steady,
insistent,
certain.

Coming into oneself
is sacred work
the work of quietude,
still,
and even so it burns
and burns
till there is
naught but
being.

2006
Seattle

The Real Question

The real question is
how to do it?

How relate a vision
of radiant bliss
and somehow
make it visible?

How tune a voice
in such a way
the ineffable
might be heard?

How teach the lesson
learned so dear
and make it
comprehensible?

How unveil each
seeming paradox
transcending the world
of dual?

2006
Seattle

What Is the Distance?

What is the distance
from our heads to our hearts
and how do we find the way?
Cleverness, smug
in its supremacy
steadily builds a patina
intricate, beautiful,
thick
layering on like sculpted
bronze
shells of brilliant defense
is finally shattered
with heart breaking open,
open for all to see,
and there
lies the path
to freedom.

2006
Seattle

WHAT NEED?

Our seed selves
broken open
unfurl in sweetness,
blossom, fruit
what need then
our fear of breaking?

Clay, molded
by every hand and random thump
shaping our seeming solidity,
only when fired
in the heat of love and loss
do we become vessels
capable of holding
and then
that which we have always been
warm milk of compassion
comes welling from within.

2007
Seattle

Full To Brim

Someday not far
we will measure the fullness
of these days
glasses raised in celebration
full to brim,
remembering

bodies stretched too thin
events crowding, even the ones
we wanted, to a narrowing crevasse
where pressure building
more so from within
forced us through
and our hearts
were broken.

Like seeds
hitting the ground hard
shock, numbing
harshness weathered
and then some
until cracking open
sudden joy!
emerging on new wings
and thus the dawning —
we have always been
so.

April 7, 2007
Seattle

Thank You
for the Poem

I have been all morning
holding my cat,
had to restrain her
to cut her nails and oh,
the anger, but now she is back
seeking something warm and
recumbent, so we are sitting,
snuggled and I found your book
and re-read "After Kuo" * and am
loving how you put it, " Working
the puzzle...searching for
a familiar edge..."
and you know, there, at the end, after
"Multiple pieces of carrying, fitting"
in the empty space that follows
on the page
I saw,
or was it spoken?
letting go

May 26, 2007
Seattle

* After Kuo, by Marion Power

2013

There is nowhere I need to be other than where I am. Growth and change will arise out of the inner urge that is common to all of life—the longing inside that drives us to evolve, the power that fuels the necessity of our opening. Very like a plant going through its stages of development, the unfolding into growth is part of what the plant IS. No part of that growth is better than any other part of the process. Is a seed better than the leaf, than the flower or the fruit? These are simply different stages in a single flow that is life/death. All my seeming awkwardness and stumbling mirror the growth of the plant from a human perspective. It is a profoundly beautiful process that holds the paradoxical truth of life in one enormous riddle of wholeness.

To heal, I have learned that there is no need to grasp after or hide away from anything. Opportunities for growth will always arrive, bidden or not. Better to be present in the moment so the situations that come can be fully digested before I take another big bite of life. To relax and notice where I truly am, with all the feelings that are present and without any attempt to edit what is true, is my task. Then I can bring compassion to bear on what I discover and make choices that are informed by wisdom.

Mindfulness relies upon our asking, "Is it true?" If the answer to that question is "I don't know," humans have a tendency to fill in the blanks with our assumptions. Practicing mindfulness, I try to let go of the imaginary input that my mind creates, attempting to explain away my uncertainty, and simply rest in my "not knowing."

Though I may never understand why things happen I have come to a place of peace with the mystery of what IS and been able to heal the wasteland that I, myself, create when trying to rationalize that mystery. Thinking mind is a wondrous tool but it cannot resolve all of life's riddles. My heart helped me find a path of healing where reason could not follow.

While growing in awareness through mindfulness is not always a comfortable process I have found the practice to be of profound benefit in healing after trauma. As it is said, "Pain happens but suffering is optional." Wanting things to be different than they are, whether from aversion or desire, is what creates our suffering. Learning how to move toward discomfort is where we begin to learn how to make peace with what is true, letting go of imagined scenarios, wholeheartedly engaging the challenges life brings.

My definition of happiness is being at peace with what IS, grounded in the paradoxical nature of life where the horrific and the profoundly beautiful are mysteriously bound together. In response to this bewildering truth I have had to bring my best effort and deeply engaged attention to all my activities, trying to learn how to respond skillfully to the many situations that unfold. To find peace in my heart an opening was required, opening to all of life with unconditional love and compassion without imagining there is a place where peace will eventually look like I think it "should" look. Life will be what it IS, sometimes hard to bear, but I have found a way to live in the midst of difficulty with greater ease and joy through mindfulness practice.

Engaging life's challenges without judgment or the overlay of our dreams and fears is difficult work but therein lies true healing. The healing I speak of is different from the happily ever after scenario that has captivated our culture. It is so much larger even pain fits. When we tap into that larger heart source, of which we are an integral part, we can grow beyond what we ever thought possible and share in ways that might once have stretched us too far for comfort.

My life has been forever changed by the loss of my son. I will always lament our loss, but Colby's legacy has initiated a metamorphosis opening the doors of my heart and perceptions, a fact for which I am grateful. And I am grateful for all the people I have met through survivor work, and for all the significant help that has come my way over the years. For me, the most valuable lessons have always come through difficulty, for it has been in the midst of struggle that I have found my life's meaning and community.

These poems are part of my process over many years as I continue to learn how to hold with equanimity the enormous paradox that life IS. I welcome you to read them aloud and to join me in my garden, healing.

THE LIGHT WITHIN

The cracks that come to us
through living every day
send shivers
through our seeming selves
and cause us to lament
but when cracks come
that cut clear through
we wake to paradox.

Broken brings us whole
no need for fear
nor need to search
life brings it to our door.
Even if we try to hide
the message will be there.

We are the light, the root, the source
and wholly broken find
the cracks that seem to let light in
are how the light gets out.

April
2013

Resources

Online

American Association of Suicidology (AAS)
www.suicidology.org

American Foundation for Suicide Prevention (AFSP)
www.afsp.org

Forefront: Innovations in Suicide Prevention
(ForefrontUW) www.intheforefront.org

King County Crisis Clinic (KCCC)
www.crisisclinic.org

Positive Changes in the Aftermath of Loss
www.posttraumaticgrowth.com

Suicide Prevention Resource Center (SPRC)
www.sprc.org

Books

Good Medicine, Pema Chodrön (Audio Book, Sounds True, 1999)

Healing through the Dark Emotions: The wisdom of grief, fear, and despair, Miriam Greenspan (Shambala, 2004)

Loving What Is, Byron Katie (Random House, 2002)

Luminous Emptiness, Francesca Fremantle (Shambala, 2001)

Making Friends With Death: A Buddhist Guide to Encountering Mortality, Judith Lief (Shambala, 2001)

My Son...My Son..., Iris Bolton (Bolton Press, 1996)

Night Falls Fast-Understanding Suicide, Kay Redfield Jamison (Vintage, 1999)

The Power of Now, Eckhart Tolle (New World Library, 1999)

The Tibetan Book of the Dead: The Great Liberation Through Hearing In The Bardo, Francesca Fremantle and Chögyam Trungpa (Shambala, 1975)

The Tibetan Book of Living and Dying, Sogyal Rinpoche (Harper Collins, 1992)

The Wisdom of No Escape, Pema Chödrön (Shambala, 2001)

When Things Fall Apart: Heart Advice for Difficult Times, Pema Chödrön (Shambala, 1997)

Wherever You Go There You Are, Jon Kabat-Zinn (Hyperion, 1994)

About the Author

A gardener by trade, Kristen's life was undone by the tragic death of her eldest son. Writing and mindfulness meditation seemed to be all that remained intact of her former world. Both practices provided tools she needed to find her way through the labyrinth of loss. Noticing how little help was available to trauma survivors, Kristen was spurred to help raise awareness about suicide pre- and postvention. Her books, *Passing Reflections, Volumes I and II*, documenting her journey over the first two years after loss, has been revised and expanded as *Passing Reflections Volume III: Surviving Suicide Loss Through Mindfulness*.

Learn more at **PassingReflections.com**